OUTBACK ADVENTURES

OUTBACK ADVENTURES

THROUGH INTERIOR BRITISH COLUMBIA

TEXT AND PHOTOGRAPHS BY

DONOVAN CLEMSON

HANCOCK HOUSE PUBLISHERS

ISBN 0-919654-16-9

Library of Congress Catalog Card Number: 74-78342

Typesetting by White Computer Typesetting,
Vancouver, B.C.

PRINTED IN CANADA

Published by:

 HANCOCK HOUSE PUBLISHERS
3215 Island View Road
Saanichton, B.C., Canada

CONTENTS

Old water wheel, relic of early flour mill

INTRODUCTION

For many years Armstrong was the base from which I conducted my small excursions in search of interesting aspects of rural life in interior British Columbia. It is a small town in the south central part of the province to which I came as a boy from England in the spring of 1924. I have since decided that no more fortunate point of arrival could have happened. I could not now select, after forty years of experience, a better or more convenient base for journeys of exploration into the large interior part of the province. Since the first novel impressions faded I have never regarded the scenery and topography around Armstrong as very interesting, and would even describe it as almost as monotonous as the climate itself. The mountains, it is true, attain altitudes of 6,000 feet and more, but they are set back and diminished by a wide foreground of farmland. They are wooded to their summits and at present almost unravaged by forest fires, and must appear to travellers coming from the Kootenay in the east and the Selkirks in the north as low hills.

The monotony of the climate around Armstrong is a feature that seems to please the majority of the inhabitants. Certainly ideally suited for the business of this agricultural community it offers little to those who need the stimulation of erratic weather. The general absence of wind in the locality renders the winters more tolerable to those of tender susceptibilities than the often snowless areas of the southern valley, where fresh winds blowing off Okanagan Lake make a mockery of more moderate thermometer readings.

There are no hurricanes, no cyclones, no eruptions, and only a few brief disturbances that might be described as storms. When reports of the raging elements occupy first place in press and radio Armstrong never makes the headlines with exciting stories of washouts, earthquakes, slides, floods and tidal inundations with all the accompanying property damage.

Undoubtedly this boring sameness of scene and climate drove me to seek the variety I needed by exploring whenever possible the varied landscape, which, I soon discovered, surrounded the locality to which I was practically rooted at first by my 365-day-a-year job as chore boy on a dairy farm.

Armstrong is situated near the northern end of Okanagan Valley on a natural divide between the Columbia and Fraser systems. It is just out of the dry belt but not in the wet belt, a sort of in between region which has the advantages of both and the drawbacks of neither. Its geographical position sets it in the centre of a region endowed with the most surprising contrasts in topography and scenery and it lies almost at the crossroads of major travel routes leading north, south, east and west.

North leads to the Shuswap country and the Selkirks, whose sharp rock pinnacles are subject to some of the heaviest snowfall in British Columbia. South takes you to the other extreme, the arid landscape of the southern Okanagan, almost a desert, with sagebrush, cactus and greasewood dotting a terrain which is the congenial home of the rattlesnake. East leads to the Kootenays, a rugged up-on-end country divided by long fiord-like lakes and riddled with old mines, while the western route sets you, in an hour, in the Thompson country and the open grasslands of Douglas Lake and the Nicola Valley.

These routes lay open and inviting in my youth, but for years I was unable to take advantage of them.

Anchored to a barn full of cows whose wellbeing required that they be milked twice a day it was not possible to make more than day trips in search of scenic variety, generally on Sundays with instructions to be back by 6 p.m. But even with such limitations the local beauty spots soon became familiar. I remember horse and buggy trips to the head of Okanagan Lake and the then novel landscape of bare, burnt-up hills reflected in quiet water. By the same means of transport the scenic attractions of the Shuswap River a mere ten miles from Armstrong were investigated, and the diminutive charms of Salmon River, a rippling stream a dozen miles over the hills. Swan Lake, Otter Lake and Davis Creek were other points that lured me on my Sunday excursions. Water, it seems, was the main attraction, that commodity being almost absent at Armstrong, represented only in a dismal way by a length of ditch which had straightened the erratic windings of Deep Creek through a large flat of black and productive vegetable land.

Excursions by automobile were few and were provided by friends and the farmer for whom I worked, who liked to take his occasional holidays at some quiet spot well within the range of a Model T. But even these not always reliable means extended my effective radius to thirty or forty miles and I became acquainted with the undisputed beauties of Kalamalka Lake, Mabel Lake, the Shuswap country and the quiet shores of Mara Lake.

I was taking photographs at the time in a haphazard sort of way and knowing little of the technical side I only rarely achieved satisfactory results. The limited success I did have encouraged me to continue, however, with considerable waste of film and darkroom materials, until I had learned one of the basic requirements for successful scenic photography: to be there at the right time. This knowledge, and the habit of seeking out interesting scenes and landmarks was most useful when my technical ability had developed to the stage where I could make presentable photographs.

Three years on a dairy farm and the devilish security of a job which demanded my presence every day of the year prompted, or rather, intensified, a desire for a more adventurous and stimulating life. I headed for the Cariboo, on foot, accompanied by my boyhood friend, George Stephens, who despised the life of a chore boy as practised on a neighbouring farm. Even with this slow method of propulsion I was amazed at the complete change of scene achieved in the first two days. The solid, long-established chequerboard of farm land of the North Okanagan had given way to more open country, primitive and wild — the Thompson Valley with a sparse flora adapted to a precipitation of seven to ten inches a year. For the first time I saw the sagebrush, covering but not concealing an eroded terrain furrowed and gouged by sudden and brief summer rainstorms. In this tortured landscape solitary pines extended their crooked limbs and contorted junipers writhed like snakes out of the rocks, mocked by the useless Thompson River, a blue thread as unattainable as a mirage, in its deep and rocky canyon.

This was a new British Columbia to me, very different from all the pictures I had seen which usually depicted forested mountains, lakes and orchards; but I subsequently learned that this dry-belt country covered many hundreds of square miles. It had a strange fascination for me, a condition that has persisted to the present time. This country seems ageless, and although it has been occupied by white people since 1860 the signs of their industry are lost in the immensity of the general scene. The ranches are many miles apart so that their irrigated hay fields appear as oases in a desert of rock and parched earth, and the fences that straggle here and there across the terrain seem to intensify rather than ameliorate the general emptiness of the scene.

North of this interesting landscape lies the Cariboo, a region of heavier precipitation than the dry-belt and consequently of different aspect, being moderately timbered. But the same ageless feeling is there, due, I am inclined to believe, to the general sparsity of settlement. There were no sections of country divided into neat little squares as in the Okanagan; the ranches were well spaced, with much rough and undeveloped country in between. Many of the houses and barns were built of logs, and a generally old-fashioned atmosphere prevailed.

We worked for Jim Bishop at Bonaparte Ranch near Clinton and at Mound Ranch where a young cowpuncher type, Doug Walters, was in charge. Then we travelled west through Canoe Creek, and crossed the Fraser into the Chilcotin country. This country was wilder than the Cariboo, and more sparsely settled. The big ranches were like small villages, surrounded by their empty dominions. We were employed by a small rancher at Big Creek for a while and became acquainted with mosquitoes and jack-pines. Then we went on to Chilco Ranch in the Chilcotin Valley and stayed there for a year.

During this period the spell of the country really took a hold on me. I was impressed by the size of Chilco Ranch and the ruggedness of the natural features. One of the ranch meadows, at which I spent a winter feeding cattle, was fifty miles from the home ranch, on the plateau country with a near view of the glittering peaks of the Coast Range. Later I spent several seasons prospecting in those mountains.

Working on the ranch was a great improvement on dairy farming. I now had a working day of only ten hours which left me with more free time than I had ever had. There was no work at all to be done on Sundays. Altogether I spent two years working on Chilcotin ranches and would have probably remained longer if the Great Depression hadn't disrupted my plans. I was forced to retire to

Cariboo ranch with log buildings and corrals near Loon Lake, south of Clinton.

the North Okanagan where I was better acquainted, and hole up in a shack until the opportunity arose to invest my modest stake in an undeveloped farm, such property being extremely cheap at the time.

Marriage followed, and I found myself tied once more to milk cows, but with the advantage that I could ignore their feelings about being milked regularly now I was the boss. My wife, Doris, and I first made Sunday trips in the surrounding country by team and democrat, or sometimes with friendly neighbours who were mechanized in a primitive way. Later, after acquiring a son, two daughters and an old touring car we began seriously to explore the valley and its precincts, and in ever widening circles sought out the beautiful, the picturesque and the unusual, a practice that has continued to the present time.

THE SHEEP CAMP

One of the annual events of our early farming days was the summer sheep drive that clogged local roads and brought traffic to a halt in the little towns of Armstrong and Enderby through which one large band passed, followed by shepherds — or sheepherders as we prefer to call them in the west — dogs and pack-horses with camping gear. This was the Palmer band from Okanagan Landing heading for summer pasture on the high mountain ridge north of Enderby known as Hunter's Range. Another large band left the Vernon area and travelled east to pasture in the Monashee mountains, while the Westwold sheepmen moved by easy stages to the high mountains behind the north shore of Shuswap Lake.

Apart from the fact that these same bands returned by the same routes each September with heavier fleeces and larger lambs we knew nothing of their summer wanderings. We could see the distant mountains where they ranged, it is true, but we had no means of following them there, for the loggers at that time had not conquered all the mountains with their road-making equipment. Only pack trails led to the alpine meadows; the sheep filled the roads for a while, then disappeared into the bush to follow trails only they and the shepherds knew. We used to run into the Palmer band when returning from summer picnics at Mara Lake. We were halted in the road while the sheep surged by; the children loved the lambs, admired the cleverness of the dogs, and said hello to the shepherds. Eventually we got to know the Palmers, and son Bill offered to take me to the range in his four-wheel-drive vehicle — for by this time there was a road of sorts up the

mountain — to see how the shepherds lived. The resulting memorable trip is the subject of the following story.

Bill Palmer turned his truck off the road into a narrow logging track and shifted to four-wheel drive. "Fourteen miles to the top," he informed me, "and climbing every foot." An hour and a half later and 5,000 feet higher the climbing ceased. I wasn't sorry. Several times during the ascent our feet were level with our ears as the truck groaned up an extra steep pitch, yet Bill indicated an almost vertical track off to the side and observed "The old jeep road — it was wicked." I understood he considered the present road first rate.

We had arrived at Bill's summer sheep pasture on the top of Hunter's Range, a thirty-mile ridge of alpine country at about 7,000 feet elevation. Here the high, rich meadows were dotted with thick clumps and islands of balsam, the timberline tree of southern British Columbia. Along a faint track over the undulating grassland the truck continued and just before sunset a column of smoke rising near a dark thicket of balsams indicated the position of the sheep camp.

"All's well," said Bill, spotting the smoke, and soon we topped a knoll and saw the flock, or band, as sheepmen say, in a hollow, grazing towards camp.

The Palmers' sole interest is in sheep. On the home ranch at Okanagan Landing they grow alfalfa hay in the irrigated fields, producing three crops annually. Operations are mechanized and handled by the family without outside help. Here the band is wintered through until after lambing. A rugged mountain pasture at Six-Mile Creek on the west side of Okanagan Lake provides spring and fall grazing and the lush alpine meadows of Hunter's Range support the sheep during the hot summer months of July and August, and part of September.

Cotton grass rings a mountain pond on the high sheep range near Palmer's camp.

Summer grazing is limited only by the weather. The band is moved up the mountain as soon as conditions are favourable. Actually it is spring on the heights. The snow has just melted and the long, sunny days of mid-June bring forth a profusion of flowers. The sheep remain until driven down to the valley by the September snows. During the time the 1,800 sheep are on the mountain they make little impression on the rich and extensive herbage. There are many meadows left untouched where one walks knee deep through the grass and flowers. Always it is the coming of the snow that drives the sheep from the mountain, never the failing of the grass. Bill says it is unexcelled sheep country and the band comes off the mountain in the peak of condition. Without exception the lambs are fat and top grade. Cool breezes temper the summer heat and the thick clumps of trees provide shelter during storms. At such times no sheep are visible in the meadows because the band is lying snug in the dense balsam.

On the occasion of my visit Bill was making his weekly trip to the mountain to bring supplies to shepherd Bob Middlemiss who stays with the band all summer. As we drove up to the tent the two dogs came bounding out to meet us and Bob stirred up the camp-fire. The sun now touched the western rim and had disappeared before we finished unloading the truck. We were still occupied when the band, which had been grazing near, came in to the bed ground. There was a sudden rumbling of the earth, a tinkling of bells and bleating of lambs as the close packed sheep moved in and settled themselves for the night. Taking the hint, Bill and I looked around for a rock-free site to lay our sleeping bags before complete darkness fell.

The smoke from many forest fires shrouded the valleys but on the mountain top the air was clear. Under the bright stars we sat around the camp-fire, and the talk, naturally, was of sheep, bear, cougar, getting lost and the

On the mountain range the band comes in to the bed ground just before sunset.

advantages of living on a mountain. Bill had intended to move the sheep a few miles farther along the ridge but Bob, the shepherd, said no, they were doing fine, there was ample pasture yet in the vicinity of the present camp and nothing would be gained by moving.

Bill said to me, "Bob knows sheep. He's had forty years' experience with them and when he says there's no need to move camp, well, we just don't move."

"We don't herd the sheep," he continued. "We let them roam where they will on the mountain. Wherever they are they always start back towards camp in the late afternoon. They know if they don't come we send the dogs to fetch them and the dogs bring them right along, pretty smart. The sheep don't like that. We don't corral them at night. They always bed down in the open, then if it rains they move to clean ground so the bed ground doesn't get foul."

From the darkness beyond the glow of the fire came the night sounds of the drowsy flock. A thirsty lamb called to its mother as it anxiously tried to find the right ewe among nine hundred. A contented ewe belched and a bell tinkled suddenly, startling and clear.

We began to discuss bears. Bob said he hadn't been bothered at this camp so far although there were plenty of bear signs when the sheep moved in. A large patch of ground on which the band was at present bedded down had been churned up by grizzlies digging out marmots. Bill's description of his first encounter with a wounded grizzly made us laugh. He was a youth at the time, helping to herd his father's sheep on the same range, and the bear came out of a balsam thicket straight at him. Bill was badly scared and shot off at top speed. The shepherd dropped the bear but Bill didn't know this and gathering all his resources he put on a terrific burst of speed and disappeared from the vicinity. Bill said neither of them had any supper that evening; he was too frightened to eat and the shepherd couldn't eat for laughing.

Once, when a former shepherd of the Palmers was camped at the Six-Mile Creek range a marauding cougar was chased by the dogs and, evidently confused, bounded into the tent and landed on the sleeping shepherd. He awoke, and thinking the intruder was one of the dogs, chased it out of the tent with a cuff and a few suitable remarks. For a brief moment the fleeing animal was outlined in the tent doorway, and seeing its huge form the astonished shepherd realized he had just been at grips with a cougar. He had suffered a few scratches and his sleeping bag was torn.

That night, on my chosen piece of rock-free ground, I watched the serene stars and reflected that the shepherd's life is essentially the same today as it always has been, as long as man has kept sheep. I recalled the story in Genesis of Jacob and his flocks and how, when the brothers were out on the range, Jacob sent Joseph, the youngest son, to check up on the sheep camp: "Go, I pray thee, see whether it be well with thy brethren, and well with the flocks; and bring me word again." Here, on a British Columbia mountain, 5,000 years later, was a similar scene: the flock lying close under the stars, Bob the shepherd snoring in the tent, and Bill, like Joseph out from the home ranch to inspect the sheep, sleeping like a log in the lee of a boulder. Only the four-wheel-drive truck looming large against the night sky introduced a modern note.

The morning routine in camp was brief but enjoyable. Bob filled our cups with some strange nectar, the chief ingredients of which seemed to be coffee and wood smoke. He put a pan of bacon on the fire and we watched with tongues hanging out as he turned each sizzling slice. After breakfast Bill, accompanied by the two dogs, walked through the band looking for a ruptured ewe that needed treatment. He soon found it and held it while Bob made rapid repairs with needle and thread. With the sun now well up in the sky the sheep decided it was time to start for pasture and they were soon fanning out belly deep in the rich grass of a meadow east of camp. They would spend the day grazing and resting, grazing and resting, and when the shadows began to lengthen start to drift back towards camp.

Bill watched them go. There was nothing he would have liked better than to stay on the mountain with the band, but there was a third crop of hay coming along

Fat lambs from the Palmer's band, just off the mountain range, being driven into nearby Enderby for shipment.

down at the ranch and he would have to return that evening. Bill said the lure of this high country was strong. As a young man he had spent many summers on the mountain with the band and now the balsam and the heather were in his blood. When the hay was safely stacked he would come back and spend a week or two on the mountain.

That was in 1958 when the big sheep bands on the roads were still a fairly common sight and a temporary hindrance to traffic on their various travel routes. Hayward Brothers of Westsyde up the North River above Kamloops were at the time running 5,000 sheep, the largest operation of its kind in British Columbia and they ranged the mountainous country on the other side of the Fraser west of Clinton for summer pasture. The spring and fall migrations of their bands occupied many weeks. They used unfrequented tracks though, drifting leisurely through the hilly country north of Kamloops Lake via Criss Creek and Back Valley to emerge on the Cariboo Road for a short stretch before plunging into the bush again at Clinton heading for the canyon ferry at Big Bar Creek.

On numerous occasions I ran into their bands when on back road exploration in the Cariboo and Deadman Valley and on their spring range at Lac du Bois back of Kamloops. They were always good for interesting photographs but the pictures I most wanted to get for some years eluded me. I was anxious to photograph the bands making the crossing of the Fraser at Big Bar Ferry, but sheep are unpredictable travellers, and I, a farmer, had not unlimited time to follow them. For years I was baffled but I finally arrived at the right place at the right time. The story of the crossing is told in a later chapter.

Lookout on Mt. Begbie in the Cariboo. It's not a mountain, really, just a knob on the plateau, but it commands a wide view in all directions.

MOUNTAIN WATCHERS

Some of the earliest day-trips made from our farm near Armstrong took us to the top of several of the apparently low mountains that form the uneven horizon of this part of the interior. Such vantage points have been utilized for years by B.C. Forest Service as sites for fire-watchers' lookout towers. These may be approached over steep and tortuous roads which in most cases permit one to drive to the very summit of the mountain. The pampered motorist is thus indulged with extensive map-like views of the valleys far below, a pleasure previously reserved for the more energetic mountaineer. The forestry lookouts with their solitary hermits are generally perched about 4,000 to 5,000 feet above valley levels, in a different world from the farmer in the valley; and this difference in elevation alone is sufficient to render the trip up the mountain an exciting and interesting event.

Our nearest mountain lookout was at Aberdeen Mountain — more popularly known as Silver Star — near Vernon, a mountain of 6,300 feet. The lookout tower itself was not visible from our farm, as a shoulder of the mountain intervened, but we often wondered about the little eyrie and its lonely occupant when thunder clouds hung low over the mountain and lightning struck along the ridges. It was one of the most accessible lookouts, being close to Vernon, and was reached by a road which joined Highway 97 in the valley just north of that town. Typical of these mountain tracks, the route left the valley farms and orchards to climb through a scattering of mountainside clearings made by overoptimistic settlers of early days, getting steeper and narrower as it progressed. The

Terrace Mountain lookout above Okanagan Lake is well above timber on the bald mountain top.

natural transition of flora in a 5,000 ft. climb makes these mountain trips particularly interesting, and the Silver Star road revealed the usual sequence from yellow pine and Douglas fir at the base up through the region of jack-pine and larch to the spire-like summit trees, the spruce and balsam which are always dominant at the higher altitudes. There were new smells to be savoured, unusual flowers and shrubs, and birds, not strangers, but known in the valley only as winter residents. As a rule the air on the mountain tops was keen and fresh, but there were annoyances in the form of various biting flies that seemed to attend every picnic on the heights.

We followed the rough tracks to several mountain lookouts in our vicinity. Terrace Lookout on the west side of Okanagan Lake required more than usual effort to attain as the road ended some distance below the summit, leaving the final rocky stretch to be covered on foot, but Tuktakamin Mountain near Falkland proved accessible to a determined driver. We made several trips to Tuktakamin, and got to know the watchman, Joe Hambrook, fairly well. He could glance down from his lookout to his little farm, a clearing in the forest, and spot his daughter's white goats in the pasture. His family could see his light at night, like a star resting on the peak. Later, we extended our investigations to lonely lookouts in the Cariboo, Chilcotin, the Skeena and the Slocan country, and in every case found interesting men at their summer occupation — watching over the surrounding forest to spot and report the first sign of smoke.

These men didn't mind living alone yet they all were glad to receive visitors. Location, of course, decided the degree of their isolation, for those like Silver Star in the vicinity of a much-travelled highway would attract many more people than the more remote lookouts where a custodian could easily pass the summer without company other than that represented by the regular visits of the ranger. Hamilton Lookout in the Merritt area is one of these isolated posts, and there I went to get the story of the daily round of a lookout man in the dry season. It was an easy day-trip, in 1958 — before the water bomber had introduced a mild diversion into the lookout man's monotonous vigil.

Perched in his eyrie on Hamilton Mountain, Ed Slater cocked an attentive ear to the north. The sound he heard was unexpected as it was unmistakable: the distant groan of some motor vehicle labouring in low gear. He stepped out on to the catwalk that surrounded his tower and located the sound in the timber far below the lookout. Somebody was driving up the steep and twisting road to the tower. Visitors!

Ed had spent a lonely summer. Isolated Hamilton Mountain is one of a network of fire lookout stations maintained by B.C. Forest Service in interior British Columbia. It is in a lonely situation in the Merritt district in Nicola Valley and commands a magnificent view of mountains in all directions. Ed had come up early in the summer to take the place of the previous incumbent, a young man fresh from college, who, shortly after being installed, had apparently put to himself the question, "O solitude, where are thy charms?" — sensed a negative response, and promptly resigned.

On this golden September day Ed was in just the mood to receive visitors. The summer had been a monotonous one for him. Not a wisp of smoke had risen in the vast circle under his surveillance, but here and there were scars left by previous fires, reminders that this summer-long vigil could not be relaxed. Visitors had been few. He could count the occasions on one hand, using only two fingers. Once there had been the inspector. His neatly completed report was pinned to a wall in the living quarters. It was a very good report, both tower and occupant having been found in satisfactory condition. "Floor," it read, "swept; windows, clean; bed, made; utensils, clean; clothing, neat; occupant, clean shaven." In conclusion was the pencilled remark, "very well maintained," and a note, "road needs grading," a curious comment indeed, since all roads to lookouts need grading.

Hamilton is not a high mountain, but at 4,900 feet its crest projects well above the surrounding country, which in the immediate neighbourhood is mostly open range. Southward, a parklike area dotted with small lakes lies like a map far below. Northward, rolling, treeless range-land extends for many miles to rising ground with dense

Joe Hambrook, watchman on Tukkakamin Mountain, hooks rugs in his spare time on the breezy mountain top.

forest in the dim distance. This is the domain of the great Douglas Lake ranch. Beyond, rise mountains and beyond these more mountains, so the full circle of the horizon is notched with mountains, fading at last into the haze. In this ocean of peaks dwell Ed's neighbours, his fellow lookout men. In clear weather he can spot some of the nearer towers, within 30 miles, through his binoculars. He can see Tuktakamin, 5,811 feet, and Greenstone, 5,844; Terrace, 6,248, lies behind an intervening peak, but Promontory is visible to the south. Black Knight and Livingstone are also among his immediate neighbours.

During my visit to Hamilton, Ed told me of his four month sojourn in the lookout. "It's lonely up here," he admitted, "and it's been monotonous. No fires to report; the quietest season for years; but I've got some nice neighbours." He waved a hand at the distant peaks. "Weekdays," he continued, "we can use the radio only for business, but Saturdays and Sundays we can talk to any of the lookouts and, believe me, there's some gabble and chatter going on. Fellow way up in the Cariboo telling about the fishing; somebody else claiming the huckleberries are ripe in his locality. You hear everything that's happening all over the place, everybody's talking."

"But what happens," I interrupted, "if you want to report a fire with all this gossip going on?" "Chase 'em off the air," Ed replied. "You grab a tin pan and hammer it with a spoon near the transmitter; you've got the floor; then you make your report." Ed's face was solemn as an owl's as he made this statement, but I made a mental note to check it with the assistant forest ranger later. Ed said he'd been waiting to clear the air all summer but the opportunity hadn't arisen.

For a conscientious lookout man the day starts early. Ed says the best time to scan the country is before sunrise. At this time distant smoke may be more easily detected as haze is at a minimum. At 7.00 a.m. the district dispatchers start calling each lookout to receive the morning report, which includes information on the weather, direction and velocity of wind, visibility and any observed smoke. First call is made by the Penticton dispatcher to lookouts in his district, followed by Princeton, then Kelowna; and at 7.18 Ed is ready to make his report, for which he is allowed one minute, when the Merritt dispatcher makes contact. Cooking and housework occupy a considerable part of the day; but while performing these tasks Ed can keep an eye on his forests through the windows which completely surround his tower. Periodically through the day he studies his familiar world through binoculars and at 7.18 p.m. the Merritt dispatcher calls for the evening report. After a last careful look around just before dark, Ed retires for the night.

The Hamilton lookout tower is sturdily built and is anchored to the rocky summit with stout cables attached to eye bolts sunk into the bedrock. At times terrific winds sweep the mountain, and Ed said his first storm scared him badly. He thought the tower was going to blow away. His quarters are furnished with cook stove, bed, chair and table, cupboards for food and utensils, and the radio transmitter and batteries. The instrument called the firefinder is located in the middle of the room; by sighting through it the operator can report the exact bearing of a fire. Once each week the assistant forest ranger, stationed at Merritt, brings supplies and fresh water to the lookout.

A terrifying experience for any lookout man is a big thunderstorm. Lightning strikes often on the mountains, frequently starting fires. The lookout towers are situated on the highest and most exposed peaks, therefore making ideal targets for lightning; consequently they are very well grounded with metal cables and most of them fairly bristle with lightning conductors. During a thunderstorm the lookout man must on no account venture outside his tower. He must disconnect his radio or telephone and wait out the storm. There he stays; alone on the mountain top in his tiny refuge, stricken with awe at the frightful tumult going on around him.

The previous year a week's course of instruction was arranged for lookout men. From their 32 mountain tops they were flown to the ranger station at Kamloops. The course commenced on June 24th when the whole of southern British Columbia was soaked with the June rains and the fire hazard was nil. Instruction was given in fire spotting, the use of the firefinder, map reading and operation of the radio. To many, the most interesting part of this innovation was meeting colleagues known to them previously only by their voices on the radio, a limitation which had not, however, prevented fast friendships being formed in the past. Bob Murray, over on Promontory, had been a "voice" for years and years. He was the man to report fires to on Saturdays and Sundays, as Promontory was in communication with Merritt by telephone. Now he was exhibited in the flesh to 31 pairs of curious eyes. Ed said he enjoyed the course and was glad of the opportunity to meet the other "voices." He asked me if I knew any of them, and I mentioned the few I had visited. Earlier in the summer I had called at the Mount Begbie lookout by the Cariboo Road near 83 Mile House, and met the occupants, Mr. and Mrs. Grant. I recalled how I had admired their collection of huge, fat garter snakes. These reptiles were writhing over the granite rocks around the lookout tower enjoying the warm sunshine after a spell of showery weather, while Mr. Grant watched their movements with keen interest. These fellows were the largest and most thriving lot of garter snakes I had ever seen. Mr. Grant pointed out to me, with justifiable pride, a fine specimen over four feet long gliding out from under a scrubby juniper bush.

It is natural enough for the lookout men to encourage the wild creatures around their lonely posts but they cannot all have snakes. Ed, on Hamilton, has to make do with chipmunks. Anyone who has watched these lively little animals knows how entertaining their antics can be, and Ed's chipmunks did their best to cheer his lonely days. Away over on Aberdeen Mountain near Vernon the watchman maintains a salt lick for the deer. Aberdeen is a ridge-topped mountain, and the deer seek the cool winds that sweep over the summit on the hottest summer days. At Terrace lookout on the west side of Okanagan Lake the special friends of the custodian are Canada jays (now renamed grey jays).

Not all the lookouts are as isolated as Hamilton. The Grants, on Begbie, get many visitors during the fire season; at the time of my visit they had almost one thousand names in their visitors' book. Their so-called mountain is a granite mound rising only about 200 feet above the Cariboo Plateau, which is 4,000 feet in elevation at this point. The white lookout building is plainly visible to travellers northbound on the Cariboo Road, and many of them stop to make the short climb. Despite its insignificant height, Begbie commands a very wide view, as the plateau is almost flat in this area. The Grants claim a visibility of 80 miles in clear weather. Surprisingly, Terrace lookout gets a fair number of visitors although it is not close to a good highway. The access road, or track, climbs almost 5,000 feet in its 14 twisting miles and the last mile must be covered on foot unless the visitor has a four-wheel-drive vehicle, yet the watchman finds it worthwhile to keep a visitors' book.

Ed, in his lonely post on Hamilton Mountain, says he would get stage-fright if he had as many visitors as the Grants; but he admits it would be nice to occasionally see somebody besides his chipmunks and the owl that sits on the railing of the catwalk of the tower and hoots at him when he is in bed.

THE RANCHER'S WAY

Not all our country excursions were inspired simply by the desire to travel and explore, or the wish to escape from the confines of our own valley. A chance friendship formed by schoolboys led eventually to our "discovery" of Deadman Valley and a byway which was to become as familiar as our own back roads. Shortly after we became acquainted with Jim and Josephine Allan they left their farm at Armstrong to take over some family property, a ranch in the dry-belt near Savona where, as Jim said, they would be far removed from traffic noises and other objectionable manifestations of civilization. Josephine wrote letters, and we learned for the first time about the fascinating physical features of Deadman Valley where their ranch was situated.

There were, she told us, strange pillars or hoodoos, and rocky spires crowning eroded volcanic formations; richly coloured rock outcrops and vertical cliffs of rimrock banded with the strata of ancient lava flows. Almost desert-like, the landscape was softened by sage and juniper, but the Deadman River brought a measure of fertility to the centre of the narrow valley. Strung along this centre line a few neighbouring ranches showed startling patches of green where soil and irrigation water happened to be contiguous. There was an Indian village in the lower part of the valley and a deserted gold mine at the head where the Allans ranged their cattle. A longing to see this remarkable valley possessed us, so when an invitation came to visit the Allans at their ranch we hunted up an obliging neighbour to look after our cows and chickens, and took off for the dry-belt.

35

Actually, it wasn't far away. A mere 120 miles separated our farm from the Allans' ranch but the change in scenery was striking. The checkerboard pattern of fields in the North Okanagan emphasized the tame aspect of established settlement, a condition which has never yet subdued the ranching country. The very nature of the drybelt precludes dense and even settlement, so that much of the original landscape is preserved in its wild state. There have been modifications, of course, such as the replacement of much of the early bunchgrass by sagebrush, due to heavy grazing, but the sage itself is now characteristic of the Thompson Valley and truly compliments the wildness of the scenery. The dry-belt scene is well known to many who travel the Trans-Canada Highway which threads the valley, along with railways, power lines and other distracting elements. The clutter of modern progress brushes the old-established roadside ranches, but back in the hinterland the scene is little changed from early times. Side roads such as the track to Upper Hat Creek which turns off the highway some miles west of Ashcroft Manor, and the Deadman road running north off the highway a few miles west of Savona lead one to quiet retreats where the business of ranching — in a small way — has been carried on for a century by men and women who needed the freedom to breathe pure air and ride the unfenced ranges.

None of the ranchers in Deadman Valley could tell me how it got its unusual name. It seems improbable that the presence of a body in the locality could have been deemed a suitable reason for the designation as such objects must have been common enough in gold rush days when most interior place names originated. It is possible that a pioneer miner or fur-trader passed on his own surname to the river and its valley, for the surname Deadman is not unknown in Canada. In support of this theory a wall map of British Columbia printed in 1884 designates the river, Deadman's Creek.

After a number of visits to the valley I began to regard it as a miniature or model of the large interior ranching country. It has all the attributes and most of the features of the larger scene, the weathered log buildings and corrals, the fences, the rocky terrain, the sagebrush and cactus, the green meadows by the river, the Indian rancherie, and even the high rimrock so typical of the Cariboo and Chilcotin scene. Then there is the old gold mine at the head of the valley and a few small lakes in the upper reaches. It seemed to me that the Allans typified the ranching people who were born to the country and lived their lives in the traditional rancher's way. Their outlook on life was common to all the ranching people I had known, and although their domestic arrangements, before the days of hydro, were often primitive, they envied no one, and would not trade places with the most prosperous in civilized society.

The following story tells of the Allans' small enterprise. It can be duplicated many times throughout the ranching country where the "little man" who needs plenty of room to breathe, still retains his independence.

Seven inches annual precipitation isn't much — not enough for dry-farming, as many abandoned homes will testify in the interior valleys which compose that interesting region in British Columbia known as the dry-belt. But the ranchers have been established there ever since the eighteen-sixties when the Cariboo gold rush touched off an invasion into an area which was previously the preserve of the fur traders and the Indian tribes with which they did business. Stockmen were quick to recognize the peculiar advantages of this dry country, and the ranches they established endure to the present day, a sure vindication of their judgement. Not all the dry-belt valleys are limited to a mere seven inches of moisture. Variations up to ten inches occur without making much difference to the appearance of the landscape. Naturally, there is much

Allan ranch scene, Deadman Valley.

open country supporting sparse grass, and large tracts are spotted with sagebrush and prickly pear. Isolated ponderosa pines give some sections the appearance of park lands. Originally bunchgrass was the predominating forage.

The valleys are dry, but the hills which enclose them receive enough moisture to support luxuriant growth in forest and wild meadows. At about 3,000 feet the tree line comes in and it is above this elevation that the ranchers find their summer range. These forested mountains and plateaus are the chief sources of the irrigation water so necessary to the production of hay in the dry valleys where the ranches are located, and where the cattle are wintered. The appearance of these dry valleys is deceptive; although the grass is short and sparse it is actually rich in nutritive qualities and is considered valuable as early spring and fall range. In the days when fat cattle were shipped directly from the range the Thompson Valley in the neighbourhood of Savona had the reputation of producing the earliest marketable steers. It is a region of light snowfall and short, open winters, frequently remaining bare while much of the province is under deep snow. In this picturesque country British Columbia's cattle ranching originated and became firmly established. At nearby Kamloops the Hudson's Bay Company was running cattle as early as 1840, and one ranch near Cherry Creek is said to have been occupied since 1852. When the Hudson's Bay Company's exclusive licence to trade with the Indians and to occupy lands was terminated in 1858, this wide country was open to settlement. Through the valley of the Thompson and the neighbouring Nicola country the attractive grass lands were eventually taken up. Today most of it is fenced and subject to controlled grazing.

The rolling, grassy hills of the Nicola country must have been a fine sight to the pioneers who could ride unobstructed for days over the almost treeless terrain. The largest ranch of them all, Douglas Lake, now sits in a hollow of these hills, like a small village in the middle of its vast territory.

Farther north, in a region of more generous rainfall, the Cariboo and Chilcotin country aroused the interest of the ranchers and by the end of the nineteenth century nearly all the present cattle country was occupied. Gang Ranch, Chilco Ranch, Canoe Cree, Alkali Lake, Dog Creek and many others spread over a country as rugged as it is large. But besides the big ranches are many operations on a smaller scale, family affairs, so to speak, where the possibilities of economic exploitation take second place to the advantages ranching has to offer as a way of life.

It is the custom nowadays to class small operations as uneconomic and therefore undesirable. The cold figures of the accountant have frightened many a rancher, and farmer too, into the belief that he is losing money. But how many ranchers are motivated solely by the consideration of making money?

Douglas Allan checks the pasture fence on his ranch in Deadman Valley.

Josephine Allan likes the quiet freedom of life at remote Ply-U pasture.

To many, ranching is life itself, the only thinkable vocation in a country where raising cattle has been the prime interest since the time of earliest settlement.

My friends, the Allans of Deadman Valley, would laugh at the suggestion that they were ranching just for the money, and a sight of the ranch itself would preclude such a thought. It lies in a real story-book setting in a valley which retains much of the romantic flavour of the Old West. Deadman Valley opens from the Thompson Valley near Savona in an arid landscape liberally supplied with rattlesnakes, and trends north, increasing in elevation until it finally merges with the Cariboo Plateau. The lower part of the valley is occupied by Indian Reserve and about ten miles up the valley the white-painted, red-roofed church marks the location of the village. A few miles beyond the village the valley narrows to a canyon, and above this it widens to form a basin. Here, ringed by red volcanic rock, lie the sheltered meadows, buildings and corrals of the Allans' ranch.

When Jim Allan talks about helping to clear the sage-brush off the Walhachin flats for the big irrigation project which started its short and spectacular career in 1907 you realize he's been in this country for some time. His wife, too, really belongs. She is a granddaughter of pioneer rancher Johnny Wilson, a well known cattleman, who started cattle raising in the area in the early eighteen-sixties. At home in the saddle, breathing the delicately scented air peculiar to the regions of sagebrush and juniper, intimately acquainted with hills and valleys, range and meadows, the Allans are part of this country which has been their home for so long.

The home ranch consists of one thousand acres. It takes in the valley up to the rimrock on each side — an effective natural fence. The hillsides are fenced and reserved for spring grazing. About sixty acres of hay land irrigated from the river produces two crops annually.

Allan's cattle come to drink at the beaver pond in the Ply-U pasture.

There is a sprinkler system to reach the high spots. Summer range is on the plateau about thirty miles up the valley, and here the Allans own a 640 acre block of fine grazing land. They call this property the Ply U, a name, they say, which is derived from an Indian word meaning wild carrot. Now they have got the Ply U fenced and it is reserved for fall grazing after the adjoining government range is eaten down. I'd heard a lot about this Ply U, so I went up to see it before they turned the cattle in. It's rolling country with little clumps of aspen on the knolls and plenty of water. There is a beaver lake with a big lodge — Josephine likes to go there and sit, and watch the beavers. At the end of July the grass was lush, knee high in places and rich with white clover. Jim said the cattle would soon shorten it down when they got in. There are about 125 cows and heifers and of course the calves, about 90 head. They hold the cattle in the Ply U pasture during October and then bring them down to the home ranch.

This fenced pasture is an important feature of the Allans' management. Many ranchers aren't too enthusiastic about leaving cattle on the range through the hunting season, but to bring them down too early puts an unnecessary strain on the winter feed supply. The Allans solved this by fencing and remaining with the cattle. They can keep an eye on the hunters that way. Jim figures there are enough natural hazards on the range already without the added risk of rifle fire.

This happy arrangement came about as the result of the Allans' youngest son taking over the operation of the home ranch. Douglas and his wife, Dorothy, run things down in the valley while Jim and Josephine put in the summer and fall up at the Ply U. They love it up there. They've built a really comfortable cabin close to a spring in a little grove of trees. The grass is good so their saddle horses never wander far. Being right on the range they can keep an eye on the cattle, and there's time to explore the country too. Jim spends some time cleaning up hunters' dirty camps; he hates to see his scenery spoiled. Although the Ply U is only forty miles from the highway the occasional visitor who has ventured the rough valley road has exclaimed over the isolation. "How could you ever live here so far from anywhere?" exclaimed one agitated caller, fresh from the city. Josephine laughed heartily over this. She stays alone on the range when Jim goes down to the ranch to help put up the hay.

The change over from grass to grain-fattened beef has affected the Deadman Valley ranchers as well as the large operations. The Allans market calves now, in the fall, and carry only breeding cows and heifers through the winter. The present herd is mostly Hereford with a few Shorthorns. Jim likes the extra milk production of the Shorthorn, and thinks it an important point to consider when raising calves for sale. When the herd finally comes down from the Ply U the aftermath of the haymeadows provides grazing until winter feeding starts, which is generally in January. Jim and Josephine now winter in Savona but they're always eager for spring to come so they can get back to the range.

In evaluating this ranch it seems to me that all the essential ingredients for a cattle operation are here — the haylands in the valley bottom with ample irrigation water available; the open hillsides on either hand which provide early spring pasture, and the lush Ply U pasture which Jim astutely acquired in the days when pressure on range was not so great as it is at the present time. Even the natural conformation of the land is an aid to the business of ranching, for Deadman Valley is like a long trough, inclined up to the plateau range land; when cattle are driven in at the upper end they drift down on their own if required. The vertical cliffs of the rimrock, too, serve as permanent fences with the advantage of never requiring any upkeep.

But business considerations apart, the Allans appear to me ideal exponents of ranching life. No doubt this is largely due to the perfect setting of the home ranch surrounded as it is by scenic attractions of the most unusual kind, not the least of which is the high rimrock which glows crimson to the sunrise an hour before the beams slant into the valley.

The valley has changed somewhat since our first exciting visit. Hydro came with its poles and wires, and a further disruption in the form of a gas pipe-line made temporary scars. Coal oil and gasoline lamps went out of fashion and irrigation systems changed with the advent of power. But the natural features remain — under which one is tempted to include the straggling remains of the old Walhachin flume which has been there so long as to become an accepted feature of the Deadman scene. There are the five strange pillars, all in a row, only visible by careful

scrutiny from the valley road, but large and imposing when approached after a hard scramble up the mountainside. And farther up the valley a striking white rock formation known as Castle Rock rears high above the road. Sharp rock pinnacles crowd the road at Criss Creek, a stream that was worked for gold by Chinese placer miners in early days. Criss Creek enters the valley from the east through a canyon marked by a high split rock. Valley rancher Bill Philip, who is knowledgeable in such things, says the old fur trail passed through here on a traverse of the valley.

Natural productions of the valley, besides rattle-snakes which are found only at the lower end, include Lewis's woodpecker which seems to like sitting on fence posts by the rancherie, and to us on our first visit was a bit of a novelty. Then there are cougar, one of which developed a taste for the Allans' and Philips' sheep, and was tracked down and killed. The Allans lost geese to a bobcat one hard winter, and there are always coyotes and deer around. The twisted junipers lend to the valley a special character, both alive and dead, for when chopped down for fence posts — or rather, stakes — by the canny ranchers, and set securely in the rocky ground, they support fence wire indefinitely, for the wood seems indestructible. Jim Allan says he has a 60 year old juniper fence with only two posts gone — broken by fighting bulls.

Neighbours bring cattle down from the range past the Allan ranch in Deadman Valley.

FERRIES AND FERRYMEN

The dedicated explorer of back roads must inevitably, sooner or later, come to a ferry. Not the large and commodious vessel you queue up for and wait five hours for the privilege of boarding, but a small wooden contraption that is generally moored on the far side of the river you wish to cross. There are a number of these small ferries in British Columbia, getting fewer though, as routes improve, or, in the case of the Columbia River ferries, eliminated when dam builders flooded the entire route. These small ferry crossings make interesting diversions on a country trip but they can also be the cause of much inconvenience — for which the ferrymen are sorry — and some frustration for the traveller who may be unable to reach his destination due to the ferry being out of order.

There seems to be some reluctance on the part of the persons responsible to post warning signs — Ferry Not Operating — at appropriate points and thus save the innocent a fruitless journey of perhaps thirty or forty miles. No doubt, in country districts, everybody knows these things and are able to arrange their movements to suit such impediments to travel, but it is most disconcerting to the stranger who has seen the ferry distinctly marked on his map, to find his chosen route closed to him.

Interruptions to ferry services seem to be unavoidable. A common cause in the interior is flooding, which can render crossings impossible at times on robust rivers such as the Fraser, Thompson and Skeena. I was caught that way myself once on the North Thompson, but

48

Sheep going aboard the ferry at Big Bar Creek.

accepted the situation cheerfully as I realized it was my partiality for back roads that led me into the trap. A warning sign at Barriere would have kept me on the highway for Little Fort, my destination, but I chose the back road, a muddy, thirty-mile trip with the ferry crossing at the end. Driving through flood water at several low spots I finally reached the ferry and saw the rustic skyline of Little Fort on the opposite side. But the ferry was unapproachable. The ramp was deep under water and there was no possibility of crossing until the river went down.

Another and more recent incident occurred at Lytton where a ferry crosses the Fraser about a mile above the town. With friends I was exploring back roads in the

Lillooet country and had taken the track that straggles along the west side of the canyon from Lillooet to the Lytton ferry, an exciting drive — or rather, crawl — of forty-three miles. Our intention was to cross the ferry and return to Lillooet on the slick, recently resurfaced road on the east (civilized) side. We arrived in the vicinity of the ferry in time for the last crossing of the day — 5 p.m. — to find a crew of hard-hatted men just quitting work. They were evidently making some major alterations in the anchor system that holds the ferry cables, for these hung slack over the road. "Could we cross the ferry?" A fat fellow with a cheerful face, to whom the question was addressed, replied with a grin: "Oh yes. You can cross on the ferry — next week," and laughing heartily at his own wit, he hung a branch on the sagging cables to indicate the road was closed. Happy at having brought a ray of sunshine into this Public Works employee's day we turned around to tackle the forty-three mountainous miles to Lillooet. We preferred it to the highway anyway.

A proposed crossing of the Soda Creek ferry was denied us in a similar manner. Taking a fork — on a back road as usual — which was posted with a sign, To The Ferry, we travelled for a number of crooked miles only to be stopped by a barricade and the notice, Road Closed, when we thought we were near the ferry; but in this case there was no hard-hatted employee to guffaw at our predicament.

As a rule, ferrymen are easy to get along with. In the quieter situations, especially, they are often glad of the company, and indulge in conversation during the crossing. Most of them seem to like the quiet tenor of the life and a routine that flows along as easily as the river. A Skeena ferryman was formerly a Saskatchewan farmer, and the drastic change in his life pattern seemed to please him mightily. A North Thompson ferryman, in a very peaceful and secluded spot, described himself as a refugee from

Vancouver. These ferrymen live close to their work, in houses provided for the purpose, and are on call during regular hours throughout the day. If they happen to be on the opposite side of the river they can be aroused, if dozing, by beating on a conveniently placed gong, but usually they spot the vehicle at the crossing and come over for it.

One of the loneliest of these small ferries and, I think, one of the most interesting, is in the Fraser Canyon at Big Bar Creek in a very sparsely populated area forty miles west of Clinton. The traffic is very light as the road actually ends at the ferry, the wild country on the opposite side being served by trails only. It is really a rancher's ferry giving access to range land and a couple of isolated ranches whose transportation needs have always been served by pack-horses, but I didn't know this on my first visit, so drove confidently down to the ferry ramp. The ferryman hailed me good humouredly. "Want to go across?" he queried. I said I did, and the ferry was soon foaming across the stiff current of the Fraser. About midstream the ferryman said to me, confidentially: "You can't get anywhere from the other side, you know — there's no road."

"Then why are you taking me across?" I exclaimed, greatly surprised.

"You said you wanted to cross, didn't you?" he replied, with a guileless smile.

He was a very obliging ferryman. He brought me and my passengers back again, then shuttled across and back with the car so I could get photographs from the bank. Finally he took us across and unloaded us on the wild side so we could have a picnic, and promised to come and fetch us when we were ready.

On subsequent trips to Big Bar Creek I learned something of the loneliness of this ferryman's life. Sometimes

The Fraser River ferry at Big Bar Creek ferrying sheep. Slamming
the gates on a full load for the crossing.

several days passed without a passenger wanting to make the crossing. From his little house in the bottom of the canyon he can see no sign of human occupation. The only sounds he hears are lonesome sounds — the rasping sound of river sediment scouring the steel hulls of the ferry which is moored to the bank, and the sighing of the canyon wind which sometimes blows so strongly upstream that he cannot operate the ferry.

I visited Big Bar ferry a number of times, hoping to photograph the sheep crossings that were the really big events of the ferryman's year, but for a long time I was unsuccessful. My timing was not good, and being a farmer I was not at liberty to hang around the ferry for days at a time. But persistence paid, and I at last witnessed a day-long crossing of the sheep, which is the subject of the following story.

"You've hit it right this time," said the ferryman, jerking his thumb in an upstream direction. Sure enough, the sheep were coming in. Up at the bend and on the other side of the river a thin wisp of smoke indicated that the shepherds were already making camp. Dust drifted down the canyon as the sheep continued to come in. They would be bedding down soon and next morning the band would be waiting at the ferry landing, ready to cross the river.

When Hayward Ranch sheep travel between summer range and the home pasture they have to cross the Fraser, and the most convenient place to do so is Big Bar ferry in the rugged canyon which trends north from Lillooet and provides interior British Columbia with some of its most spectacular scenery. The ferry exists chiefly for the convenience of ranchers who frequently find it necessary to move stock across the river; and for a period of twenty-five years the busiest times for the ferryman were the semi-annual crossings of the Hayward bands, amounting to around 5,000 head, as they passed to and from their high-altitude summer range.

For several years I had wanted to photograph the crossing of the sheep but my timing was always wrong. I generally arrived on the scene too late. Nobody, not even the owners of the band could say to a certainty just when the sheep would arrive at the ferry. Lloyd Hayward himself told me once when I called at the ranch to seek information: "The sheep set the pace. We can't predict what day they'll cross. It depends on the speed they want to travel."

It used to be a six weeks' trek from ranch to summer range but lately the Haywards were trucking their band to Clinton, which lopped nearly a hundred miles off the drive. That left plenty of latitude, however, for the sheep to still make it a matter of guesswork as to when they would make the crossing.

I was at the ferry once on a Friday and the ferryman told me: "Sheep'll be crossing Monday. One of the boys was down here yesterday; he says they're coming right along." Well, I couldn't wait as I had to go home and put in some fall wheat. I decided to return Monday morning, which I did, having got up at 2 a.m. and driven the 175 miles to arrive on the scene shortly after dawn. But the sheep had outfoxed me. They'd crossed the previous day and were now leisurely browsing through the sage as they climbed out of the canyon.

I became a familiar figure to the ferryman. When he saw me he knew what I was looking for, and he was certainly as pleased as I was when the right moment came.

Next morning at 8 o'clock the band was waiting on the opposite bank, and Ed, the ferryman, tossed off the moorings and manoeuvered into the current to cross over and take on the first load. (Ed again! — A coincidence. Not all men who live in lonely places are called Ed.)

For convenience in handling, Hayward's sheep, when on the move, are divided into several bands each with its complement of shepherds, dogs, and pack-horses with camping equipment and supplies. The band waiting for the ferry was the first of three, spaced several days apart on the home trek from the high mountain range, and numbered about 1,700. The ewes, of course, had become accustomed to the crossing and waited patiently on the pebbly shore. There were no corrals or chutes. The dogs held the band just where it was wanted and as soon as the ferry nudged in the shepherds came aboard with a decoy ewe which they tied to the far gate. Sheep immediately trooped aboard — "Like trained pigs," one of the shepherds remarked with a grin — and when the ferry could hold no more the gate was slammed on them and the return journey begun.

These small Fraser ferries are propelled by the force of the current which glides along at a brisk eight miles per hour. The craft is attached by cables to a truck which travels on an overhead cable and when manipulated to an angle with the current is forced quite rapidly across the river. It is a thrilling ride, especially when the middle of the river is reached and the full strength of the current boils against the craft. One glances apprehensively at the overhead cable and wonders if it is strong enough to stand the strain.

The sheep took the crossing calmly, roughly one hundred to a load, sometimes more, occasionally a few less. The first bunch looked pretty small when they were liberated on the near side. To the shepherds with the band they appeared as a handful of tiny specks, almost lost in the immensity of the canyon. It made you think it would take a week to move this big solid bunch. But the ferry made a quick turnabout and came gliding back. Another load took off. After a couple of hours you could see the ferry was making an impression. The band looked

Sheep leaving the ferry on the home side of the Fraser at Big Bar Creek.

definitely smaller and the transported sheep on the near side began to amount to something. Now occurred the only unscheduled incident of the crossing. An anxious ewe, finding herself separated from her lamb which had boarded the ferry, made a courageous attempt to swim after the departing craft. She reached the strong current and was swept away like a leaf. Apparently realizing she was heading rapidly for the Pacific Ocean she turned back for shore and about half a mile below the ferry succeeded in gaining an eddy which brought her close into the bank. She made her way sheepishly back to the band.

A rancher on horseback suddenly appeared out of the sagebrush, he wanted to go across. The sheep operation was interrupted while the ferry made a trip with horse and rider. Then the cook came along with the pack-horses.

He wanted to go across so he could unload his pots and pans on the other side and prepare lunch. The sheep waited while cook and pack-horses made the crossing.

Sixteen loads and seven hours later the band was on the homeward side of the river. The shepherds had got a good count on the sheep by releasing them from the ferry a few at a time. They were pleased because they had not lost a single head on the trip so far. Ed, the ferryman would have a couple of days to recover before the next band turned up, but actually he's pretty glad to see the sheep come. It's a lonesome place down in the canyon at Big Bar.

I secured the photographs just in time. Hayward's are now out of sheep. Started in 1912 by their father, the Hayward Ranch developed into the largest sheep operation in Canada. At first the sheep were ranged in the rugged mountain country between Lytton and Cache Creek but later the range west of the Fraser was acquired, which made necessary the Big Bar ferry crossing. Hayward's had a reputation for producing early lambs, and the band used to come off the alpine range as clean as if they'd been groomed. I never saw a burr in a fleece. "But the economic end of it got us down," Doug Hayward told me recently. "We had to sell. Most of the sheep went to eastern Canada."

He didn't sound too happy about it, and I'm really sorry myself. I always felt as if I'd like to follow those sheep up into the mountains above the timber. The shepherds came out of there in the fall looking pretty rough but there's something about the look in their sad eyes that reflects the solitude of the mountains. A man would have time to think back in there.

CHILCOTIN REVISITED

Our farm operation at Armstrong allowed us a fair amount of leisure time. There were occasions when we could take several days or even a week off, provided we could locate an equally unfettered neighbour to look after our livestock during our absence. We were dry-farmers, depending on what natural moisture happened to fall out of the sky for the production of our crops. When the June rains failed, so did our second crop of hay, and we had less work, which to us was an advantage over the irrigation farmer who had to work all the time. It was the period between haying and harvest that gave us the leisure to explore a little farther afield, and each summer we were able to make several interior trips into fresh country.

My early experiences in the Chilcotin country had furnished me with indelible and ever-recurring memories of a period when that wide country, it seemed to me, had all the authentic attributes of the frontier; and I frequently wondered if the old atmosphere had changed, or the aura of romance had faded away with the passing of the pioneers. It was essential to revisit Chilcotin to see if Time had laid his heavy hands on the land and subdued it, as he had done in my own tame valley.

The memories of Chilcotin constantly returning were of long and dusty roads with many empty miles between ranches; endless miles of rail fences; old log buildings grey with dust; lonely tracks through leagues of close-standing jackpines; riders riding, accompanied by clouds of mosquitoes; distant dust clouds indicating herds of cattle being moved; and the lively ranchstead sights and sounds.

There was the painful and continuous thunder of cattle bawling for calves at weaning time; the brisk stampede of ranch hands from bunk-house to cook-house when the bell clanged for meals; the busy and exciting scenes at branding time, the ropers roping, the groups of cowboys round the branding fires, the smell of the burning hair. Not forgotten either were the bloody affairs at the dehorning chutes, springtime chores, which turned the surrounding snow crimson, and always roused the indignation of one old cowboy who had drifted up from down south, somewhere. "Why don't they do it at branding time?" Old Tex used to exclaim, "Save all this mess — all you got to do is pare the calf's horn button off and touch it with a hot iron to cauterize it." Later, Tex was elevated to the position of head rider and was able to practise this neater method of dehorning.

There were winter memories too of cold days feeding cattle, harnessing teams long before daylight and starting off with the sleigh and rack at dawn to the stackyards where the expectant cattle were already assembled — a cold job, which made you envy the two men down at the woodpile with a crosscut sawing wood. In those days the Indians made a profitable business of riding down coyotes for their pelts which were worth up to twenty-five dollars. Caught in the open in soft snow, a coyote was soon overhauled by an oatsfed horse, and many an Indian rode home daily with a coyote tied to his saddle.

Chilcotin winters were something to remember. The cold settled in the river valley, where the big ranches were situated, but on the plateau, home of the backwoods ranchers and location of some ranch hay meadows, more moderate temperatures prevailed, nothing near the sixty below and colder recorded at low spots like Redstone. I remember the hardiness of the Chilcotin Indians who were generally employed as riders on the cattle ranches and I still marvel at their apparent imperviousness to weather

conditions. They could get along in sub-zero weather in buckskin gloves and leather riding boots and sleep comfortably by a log in the snow when moving cattle in the winter.

The Chilcotin was settled somewhat later than the country adjacent to the Cariboo Road which was taken up in the eighteen-sixties. The Fraser Canyon was a barrier making for difficult access to the grassy plains of the western plateau, and ferries were the first convenient means of crossing the river dry-shod. Not until 1904 was a suspension bridge built at Chimney Creek to give effective road service to the country, but by then most of the big ranches had been established. Chilco Ranch was started in 1884; Becher's was taken up in 1886, Cotton's at Riske Creek started in 1886, and Lee's in the Chilcotin Valley 1893. The backwoods ranchers in the jackpines — or the sticks, as they say in Chilcotin — came even later. They were the independent types who needed room above everything else and didn't care if there were any neighbours within a dozen miles. A single annual trip to town — it was Ashcroft in the early days — sufficed to keep them in essential supplies. The coming of the P.G.E. into the Cariboo in 1913 shifted the supply point for Chilcotin to Williams Lake and brought the far-flung ranches within reasonable reach of civilization — if that is the correct term for the community which rapidly grew beside the new railway. Hanceville, by the Chilcotin River, was now only 65 miles from town. The ranchers' beef drives to shipping point were shortened by many days, and trucks started to roll into the Chilcotin hauling freight and the weekly mail.

The physical aspects of the country stamp it with a character unusual in British Columbia. It is high, wide, beautiful country of distant horizons with no bulky mountains to obscure the sunrise and hasten the night. There are mountains indeed, far to the west, the long line of

Anahim native village and church in the Chilcotin Valley.

snow peaks of the Coast Range which may be glimpsed from high spots on the plateau, but their very distance emphasizes the spaciousness of Chilcotin. This quality is vital to the people that settled and remained there, and was very evident to me when I went back after many years and wrote of my impressions upon my return.

I was 19 when I saw Chilcotin first. I walked in from Clinton, via Canoe Creek and Gang Ranch, and on to Big Creek, carrying all my worldly goods in a pack-sack. Thirty-one years have come and gone since then, and a lot has happened, but the memory of that great wild country never left me.

Recently I went back, curious, perhaps, to test its spell again. I found it much the same — beautiful, vast and untamed. I saw again the wide valley, bounded by low, even sides which were crowned here and there with vertical cliffs of rimrock. The river, white as milk and almost as opaque, surged through its canyon cut in the valley floor. Unaltered was the boulder-strewn plain of the plateau, fairly open in the east, but forested in the west with endless jackpines relieved by the occasional small meadow. In the dimmest distance stood the snow mountains, as the Indians call them, the long, glittering barrier of the Coast Range.

This is big, spacious country. To most British Columbians, accustomed to narrow valleys, it seems a vast land with its blue distances, and the horizon so far away that you can't even count the trees along it.

There are no paved roads, no pipelines, no railroads, no towns. The road that traverses this wide country is rough and dusty. There are miles and miles of rail fences. There are log cabins with dirt roofs, cattle, cowpunchers and corrals, just as they were when I first saw it.

At that time I had been working on a ranch near Clinton and had heard many stories about the Chilcotin — Chilicoot'n they called it — and was eager to see the country. I remember the swarms of mosquitoes that accompanied me as I walked through the jackpines. The natives said they were singing Home, Sweet Home. Later, I knew that the song of the mosquitoes meant spring in a land where life is good when the creeks and rivers are released after the long winter, and every pond and slough is alive with ducks and geese; when the snipe and curlews come, and the sun warms range and forest.

I worked for a month on a ranch at Big Creek and took my pay in horseflesh, as the rancher explained to me that everyone rode in Chilcotin. It was an old horse, I recall. Riding on to Chilco Ranch, I was hired on immediately as haying time was approaching. Chilco was running 3,000 head of cattle at that time, and ranging them right back to

Chilcotin corral scene.

the mountains about 75 miles away. During haytime about 60 men were employed, and a lot of teams. It was all hand coiling and pitching, and any cowboy foolish enough to venture in from the range was quickly put to work in the hayfield. I remember how the foreman used to chuckle about the mosquitoes. He said he never had to worry about the boys sneaking off to some quiet spot for a snooze — mosquitoes kept them on the jump. How right he was! The big stacks went up on the hay meadows steadily.

Chilco Ranch was the end of the road, and the prospectors used to outfit there before taking off for the mountains. The ranch hands would watch them loading their pack-horses, and listen to their talk, all about veins and float and drifts and footwalls. Then they would disappear in the west and we would forget about them. About the time of the first snow in the fall they would show up again at the ranch with long hair, and beards spread over their chests. It was an annual event to the barbers of Williams Lake when the prospectors came out of the mountains.

That winter I spent five months feeding cattle at Chilco's Whitewater meadows 50 miles west of the home ranch. It was high country and close to the mountains, and all winter long I could look over at the immaculate range which occupied about two thirds of the horizon. Opposite our small cabin was a twin-peaked mountain more than 10,000 feet high — Mount Tatlow, I discovered later — which fascinated me. Next spring when the sad-eyed prospectors arrived at the ranch I went with them, into the mountains. I never regretted it.

I put in a year at a ranch west of Alexis Creek, near the forks of the Chilko and Chilcotin rivers. The old-timers said that when they first came in there they didn't need hay. Cattle rustled all winter on the bunch grass which was luxuriant. But in my time, it seemed, we did little else but handle hay, putting it up all summer and feeding it out all winter. A lot of the range was then grazed down pretty short. The ranchers blamed the wild horses, of which there were great numbers.

Despite all the haying I liked Chilcotin. There is some strange attraction in that wide country that is not easily defined. Perhaps it is the openness, the solitude, and the rhythm of the swift, white river that cast the spell. Certainly there is no softness there. The winters I knew were harsh. At Redstone, a few miles from the ranch, 60 below was recorded, but up on the plateau meadows temperatures were much milder.

The spell of the country was on the horses, too. The wild bands thrived, and the Indians and cowboys used to catch them and break them for mounts. There was a saying that Chilcotin horses, taken out of the country, always go back. I encountered it several times. At Gang Ranch, where I once stopped for the night when riding south to the Bridge River country to join some prospector friends, the barn boss — after solemnly informing me of the latest tragedy, the burning of the liquor store at Lillooet — said to me: "You'll have to watch those horses, son. Chilicoot'n horses always go back." A couple of days later I was told the same thing at Lillooet when I asked directions of a local character. After reverently discussing the burnt liquor store he went on to enquire whither I was going and whence I had come, and finally he said: "Them Chilicoot'n horses you got there? You'll have to watch them, boy; they always go back." I remember meeting a man who told me he once lost some horses and followed them 300 miles before he caught them, back in Chilcotin where they were raised.

When, after many years, one returns to the country of one's youth, the mental picture from long ago is seldom quite like the actual scene. This was not true of my recent visit to Chilcotin. Driving west from Williams Lake I saw the well-remembered scenes appear, like pictures from the past. There was the same shaky suspension bridge over the Fraser that many thousands of cattle have crossed, through the years, on the beef drives to Williams Lake. At the top of the four-mile hill that winds up out of the canyon to the plateau some cowboys lay sleeping in the sun as their horses and cattle grazed nearby. It was a cattle drive, just like old times. Nowadays, of course, many cattle are hauled by truck, and the increase in truck traffic I noticed on the Chilcotin road indicated that, while

Lee's old log store in the Chilcotin Valley.

the country as a whole seemed unchanged, it wasn't sleeping. I saw trucks stacked high with sawn lumber coming out, and trucks with tractor fuel going in. The development of modern haymaking equipment has resulted in stacks of baled hay appearing on all the ranch meadows. Gone, I suppose, are the big ranch crews of former days.

The dusty road leads on westward, over a boulder-strewn plain. It is a dry season and the range is burned brown. The horizon is far away and featureless, but as the valley of the Chilcotin is approached glimpses of the distant Coast Range may be had. Those sharp mountains that notch out the sky bear on their backs the snows that feed the Chilcotin River.

Suddenly the road descends to the valley and Lee's ranch and store jolts one back into the past. Here, unquestionably, is the old, authentic touch. The same log buildings, the same log store, matching the pictures carried through the years. As far as I could see, time has been standing still at Lee's. This is reassuring, indeed, to one who sometimes thinks the world moves too fast. Past these log walls the life of Chilcotin ebbed and flowed.

I recall a certain day long ago when I arrived there with my two horses, all I owned. A large party of surveyors were outfitting and there was quite a bustle, but in spite of all the feverish activity Mrs. Lee found time to hunt me up a job, by telephone. I was a stranger but I might have been the Prodigal Son.

Beyond Lee's is the big rancherie of Anahim situated on a bench above the road and backed by a crescent cliff of rimrock. Farther on is the little settlement of Alexis Creek — all Chilcotin has to offer in the way of a metropolis — and beyond that the Chilcotin River receives its enormous tributary, the Chilko. Actually, it's a case of the tributary receiving the river, for above the junction the Chilcotin is an insignificant little stream of clear water, idling through meadows and willow thickets. It is the Chilko, many times as large, that brings the boisterous volume of opaque ice-water to the union. The Chilko and its strong tributary, the Taseko — locally called Whitewater — are fed by glaciers of the Coast Range, and in hot weather a tremendous volume of water surges through their canyons. In the late summer the salmon come, and the Indians visit the fishing places to catch them as they battle their way up-stream.

Now Indians were fishing again at Chilko River, just as they have done from ancient times. There were several camps on the flat above the canyon, each with racks of split and drying salmon, and slow fires of green wood burning beneath. Fishing is done chiefly at night, by dipping into an eddy with long-handled nets. This practice used to worry the ranchers in the neighbourhood of the fishing places, as the Indians they employed for haying would spend all night fishing and be too tired to pitch hay the following day. Apparently the Indians considered fishing to be much more important than putting up hay, although it is possible that this attitude has now been modified somewhat, as there are fewer Indians to be found at the fishing places today than in former times.

To my regret I had not time to investigate the more remote ranches, but had to turn back; but next spring when the mosquitoes in the jackpines are singing "Come back to Chilcotin," I shall probably not be able to resist the call.

The above was written in 1958 when modern innovations had still made little change in the face of Chilcotin, although the large haying crews had been ousted from the bunk-houses. Since then the beef drives have passed and the distant dust clouds on the Chilcotin road signify large trucks hurtling over the gravel. A paved surface is beginning to creep westward from Williams Lake, and a fine new steel span has replaced the old spidery suspension bridge over the Fraser that was such a bottle-neck on the beef drives. Lee's abandoned the old log store and went modern with a motel and restaurant, but enough of the old buildings remain to retain some of the old west atmosphere that was always notable there. And hydro's got into the country at last, with the familiar pattern of poles and high wires swooping along beside the road. But with all these new-fangled distractions the Chilcotin still wields a mysterious influence over the absentee. And it is big enough, it is hoped, to resist for a while the disturbing assaults of progress.

IT'S A LONG WAY TO BELLA COOLA

Away back in 1928 when I first worked in the Chilcotin country one of the most reliable topics for sustained conversation in the bunk-house was the hoped-for road westward through the Coast Range which would give the big cattle country an outlet to the coast. Solemn-faced cowpunchers, with all the assurance of experienced engineers, would plot the route and maintain arguments as to the feasibility of the project which would almost convince the most skeptical listeners.

The proposed route wasn't exactly new. Part of it had been pioneered by no less a man than Alexander Mackenzie on his great overland journey to the Pacific in 1793. Mackenzie reached the salt water at Bella Coola, the very spot later designated by the Chilcotin cowpunchers as their coast outlet. If they'd been aware of it the fact that Bella Coola was a small village isolated at the head of a 60 mile fiord, with infrequent though regular connections with Vancouver, wouldn't have bothered them. It was sufficient for the cowboys that Bella Coola was on the salt water, and a road westward would bring the Chilcotin to within little more than two hundred miles of the coast.

Already there was a road running westward through the Chilcotin to what we used to consider the back of beyond, the small settlements of Tatla Lake, Kleena Kleene and Anahim Lake; but west of the last you had to travel, like Alexander Mackenzie, across country. On the map Bella Coola looked tantalizingly close. Why couldn't the existing road be extended? You could nearly always get through with a truck as far as it went. And didn't the hermits of Tatla Lake, Kleena Kleene and Anahim Lake actually have their mail delivered to them every two weeks from Williams Lake?

I recalled these discussions of 36 years ago when I travelled westward from Anahim Lake over the road that actually did materialize to give Chilcotin residents access to the salt water, an advantage of small account compared to the benefits bestowed on the isolated Bella Coolans who previously had no land connections with the rest of the province. I thought that the cowpuncher who argued so earnestly about the necessity for the link would have been unlikely to make use of it. Certainly he would not attach so much importance to the reality as he did in the days when it was just a dream. The typical Chilcotin ranch hand and cowboy as I estimated him from bunk-house impressions in 1928 was a likeable chap endowed with unquenchable good humour. He was probably born at Soda Creek, was single, had 1.5 girl friends, smoked Bull Durham but would always accept a chew of plug or a dip of "snoose" if offered. He had travelled south as far as Ashcroft and north as far as Quesnel, and was inclined to overrate the importance of Clinton as a North American metropolis. It is doubtful if he could have made use of the Bella Coola route if it had then been available, for his radius of effective weekend travel by saddle horse would be about thirty miles, which he cheerfully covered to Saturday night dances where he met his 1.5 girl friends.

I made several trips over the Bella Coola road in the nineteen-sixties when the entire journey was made over gravel and dirt — if it wasn't mud — and weather conditions could delay the traveller, and actually bring him to a halt in the gumbo near Kleena Kleene. Now paving is beginning to creep westward from Williams Lake. Like the Romans in ancient Britain, the road-makers apparently plan to subdue the Chilcotin. Their strategy is sound. Once that long, rough, dusty road is

The new bridge over the Fraser, west of Williams Lake to Chilcotin, and, at the end of the road, Bella Coola.

converted to a sleek, black highway the oldtime atmosphere of the country will be impaired. But it's a big country, and the curious traveller will probably be able to keep ahead of the paving for many years to come. Let me describe the area between Williams Lake and Bella Coola before the road was improved.

When you turn off the pavement at Williams Lake and head westward into the Chilcotin country there are 300 miles of country roads ahead of you — gravel, dirt, rock, dust or gumbo, depending on the weather. You travel over various types of terrain, through changing scenery, through a country that is old and still retains the atmosphere of past days.

The shining new steel bridge which spans the Fraser fifteen miles west of Williams Lake fails to subdue this

The settlement of Tatla Lake in the far Chilcotin, with original dirt-roofed log cabins and tired fence in the foreground.

antique flavour which seems to be inherent in the Chilcotin, and is certainly proof against the activities of bridge builders. The original road crossing at this spectacular spot in the canyon was a narrow suspension bridge, built in 1904, a thin-looking contraption with the cable towers poised on tall masonry piers, and approaches of wooden trestle work. By the nineteen-twenties it was getting pretty shaky so load restrictions were enforced. It was then a time-consuming bottleneck on cattle drives, as only small bunches at a time were permitted on the bridge. The new span, opened in 1961, is a graceful single arch which carries a wide deck, a new link in an old route, over which heavy trucks and trailers rumble unimpeded, bringing out the products of Chilcotin — cattle, lumber and logs, from as far back as Tatlayoko Lake, right in the Coast Range.

The long, steep climb out of the canyon brings you up to the plateau level, the boulder-strewn plains with faint and distant glimpses of snowy mountains. There are rolling hills of grass where the only signs of human occupation are fences — wire fences, log fences, rail fences; many miles of rail fences. There are Russell fences, snake fences, stake and rider fences, and the nameless combinations and improvisations inspired by the lack or abundance of suitable material and the peculiar talents of the ranchers.

There are old log buildings grey with the roadside dust, dirtroofed cabins sprouting weeds, ranches, corrals, rancheries; and little country stores where you can buy anything from fancy cowboy shirts and chaps to a paperback copy of Fanny Hill.

These Chilcotin stores are remarkable institutions, and well worth a visit. Most of them date from pioneer times when the distance between them, in horse power days, perhaps represented a day's travel, and they were equipped to supply not only the normal requirements of life but the peculiar necessities of Chilcotin residents both white and native. Chilco Ranch store, 65 miles from Williams Lake, used to proudly boast: "Everything from a needle to a wagon," but this didn't prepare the stranger for the amazing variety to be found within. There were pack-saddles, lash-ropes, chaps, lariats, cinches, fancy silk shirts, big hats and cowboy boots, traps, horse-bells and rifles, and of course the indispensable items of snuff and chewing tobacco.

Lee's is an old time ranch and store 60 miles in, at the bottom of the hill where the road drops from the plateau into the Chilcotin Valley. It was established in 1893 by Norman Lee who took over the original trading post, and it has been a popular stopping place ever since. The original store was, of course, a log building and displayed many items of buckskin made by the local Indians and taken in trade. There were buckskin jackets, moccasins and richly decorated gloves, and, in the early days, superb examples of Chilcotin basket work. The Indian work is not so plentiful today, but if you're lucky you might run down the odd basket in one of these isolated stores.

In all the Lees built four stores, the most modern of which, a frame building, is across the road from the original site and adjoins a cafe and motel in which the family carry on their old tradition of hospitality. Actually, Lee's was much more than a store. It seemed to be a general employment agency as well as an outfitting depot for prospectors and surveyors. I have seen the corrals full of pack-horses, the fences sagging under the weight of the cowpunchers sitting on them, and the buildings surrounded by surveyors with high boots and shaved heads. That's how I like to remember Lee's.

At Lee's the road forks, the left hand branch leading to the ranch and post office which comprises Hanceville, then crossing the Chilcotin River to Chilco Ranch, Stone rancherie and Big Creek. The right fork continues, trending west, to Anahim rancherie, Alexis Creek, Redstone, Chilanko Forks, Tatla Lake, Kleena Kleene, Anahim Lake and finally to Bella Coola. All these names look very well on a map but don't let them deceive you. In the Chilcotin a cluster of log buildings and a row of oil drums warrant recognition on the map. A notable exception is Alexis Creek which has attained the stature of a small village and is regarded as home to a branch of the Forest Service and a detachment of the R.C.M.P. The other names, however, should not be ignored. All of them are worthy of investigation, particularly the little stores which exude the true Chilcotin flavour from every chink in their log walls. The proprietor of Chilanko Forks store has recognized the attraction these isolated emporiums have for strangers and has erected a large sign bearing an artful message containing the words: "There ain't no place like this place," which, taken by and large, and excluding the log buildings and the oil drums, is perfectly true.

By the time the traveller has reached Redstone, 95 miles from Williams Lake, he will have passed several side roads with signposts bearing fascinating names indicating that the Chilcotin has much to offer in the way of fishing and hunting, and just exploring. The signs are excellent, well painted and legible, but the tracks they point to are only roads in the Chilcotin sense, and some of them are best attempted with four-wheel-drive vehicles. I once tried the Chilko Lake road which turns off the main road 13 miles beyond Alexis Creek, and covered the 54 miles in four hours. I was told the road was "good". I found anglers there, enjoying good sport near the outfall of the lake, and glad to be camping in freedom and solitude.

A side road near Redstone bearing the inscription, Chezacut, looks inviting, especially in dry weather. It heads off through the jackpines, a fair enough track, but there are indications that the procedure in wet weather is to chop down trees and lay them in ruts. Fortunately there are plenty of trees. For 25 miles the jackpines crowd the road then, suddenly, the prospect opens up, and the Mulvahill meadows, 2,000 acres in expanse, present wide views with splendid horizons. It's one of those surprise vistas that the Chilcotin springs on you every so often.

The Mulvahills have been in there since 1907, and their collection of log buildings is imposing; the blacksmith shop itself would do justice to a village. They had to be self-sufficient, of course, in the early days when Ashcroft, 200 miles distant, was their supply point, and represented a three week journey when driving out their three-year-old steers for shipment. There was a certain amount of isolation — but not any more.

"We're not isolated," a young woman at Chezacut assured me, "we can drive out to the road in half an hour."

Remembering the trees lying in the ruts, I wondered — and yet the woman had an honest face.

Isolation, however, can more easily be associated with Chezacut school for there are no comforting log buildings in sight. It stands lonely in the everlasting jack-pines with no ranches near. Here I met a young man fresh from the city, gloomily contemplating an enormous woodpile and wondering if the elevation, 3,100 feet, actually implied the winter was long and cold enough to burn up all that wood. His first school — and he had to pick Chezacut! His charges, evenly divided between ranchers' children and natives, played around a corral full of their saddle horses.

Such side trips delay the traveller, it is true, but on the Bella Coola road the journey is more important than the destination.

And sometimes the destination seems remote, when, for instance, you spy the bi-weekly freight truck bearing down on you, the urgent message, GET THE HILL OUT OF THE ROAD, in foot-high letters above the cab. This sign, I believe, really refers to an interesting feature of the road which the inhabitants very modestly call "The Hill" and is not intended to intimidate the motorist.

Redstone has the reputation of being a bit of a cold spot in interior British Columbia, with winter temper-atures sometimes hitting the minus-sixties. The name apparently derives from an outcrop of bright red volcanic rock near the Redstone Indian Reserve about thirteen miles farther along the road. Near this spot a small Indian cemetery is so tightly packed with graves that only thin

On the road to Bella Coola, this crucifix marks a roadside Indian
cemetery near Redstone.

people can walk between the grave palings. Why this curious economy in this country of wide spaces?

Anglers will find the usual excuses for making the side trip of six miles to Puntzi Lake, 18 miles past Redstone: "Good place to break the journey," "Pretty nice for the kids," "Good camping;" all of which is strictly true, and should roll easily off the tongues of a class of people suspected of excessive lying. But such excuses will wear pretty thin by the time the traveller has reached Anahim Lake. The Bella Coola road taps a region sprinkled with fishing lakes and noted for big game. Nimpo and Anahim lakes are well regarded for the fishing but they also have scenic qualities peculiar to the high plateau country in which they are situated. On calm days they mirror the distant snowy peaks of the Coast Range and the wide Chilcotin sky, and provide many delicious vistas through groups of white-trunked aspens.

Tatla Lake, 145 miles from Williams Lake, appears as a welcome oasis after travelling many miles through unproductive jackpine country. There is an old ranch with big meadows dotted with comfortable looking hay stacks. There are log fences and very old buildings and a store. The road forks, one branch leading to Tatlayoko Lake which lies in a gap in the Coast Range 24 miles distant. Pronounced Tatlacoh, as spelled on old maps, the lake drains south to Bute Inlet by way of the Homathko River, and would be pristine wilderness if it wasn't for the sawmill on it which trucks its lumber all the way to Williams Lake. But it's a remote place to live. There are a few small ranches with miniature hay meadows. A sign, "Library" intrigued me. A track led into the bush and I followed it down to a log house cosily situated beside the Homathko River which at this point is a mere creek, and found a family living there in contentment. Fed up with city life and the routine of a coffee shop and bakery business, Jeanne and Barney Combe and their children pined for a quiet home in the wilderness. They had certainly found one at Tatlayoko Lake, for from the very door of their house they have observed moose, grizzly, cougar and lynx, while a family of mink play in the river thirty feet from their porch. The shelves of books that comprise the library are patronized by the scattered inhabitants of the region.

The 60 miles between Tatla Lake and Anahim Lake traverse elevated country well supplied with lakes and fishing camps, and with some variety in the hay meadows of Kleena Kleene which soften the bleak and rather inhospitable outlook of jackpine country. Anahim Lake itself was at one time the end of the road, a remote outpost of the Chilcotin, which maintained a tenuous communication with Williams Lake, over 200 miles distant, by way of a bi-weekly mail and freight service. On high plateau country, within sight of the shining Coast Range, and subject to summer frosts, its agricultural possibilities are limited to the production of hay on the very extensive natural meadows in the vicinity. The population seems to be a fascinating mixture of ranchers, Indians and Missionary Sisters whose white habits flash startling highlights as they move between dormitories and the school which they have established for the native children. The inhabitants are not without a certain unsubtle wit. I noticed a sign on a ranch gate: "Shut the gate, lover boy, our heifers are not so easy to catch as the one you're chasing," but whether this was a crack at the morals of the local residents or simply an attempt to draw a smile from the stray tourist I was unable to decide.

For many years the people of Anahim Lake looked westward hopefully towards the Pacific coast where, only a hundred miles away, the little fishing village of Bella Coola represented civilization in a quiet haven at the head of a 60-mile fiord known as Bentinck Arm. Actually, the lack of 40 miles of road divided the two communities, for a

A side track on the Bella Coola road leads to a school in the jackpines at Chezacot.

road ran inland from Bella Coola up the valley of the same name. The people of Bella Coola felt their isolation too, for they relied on the periodic calls of the coast ships for their connections with the outside world. They naturally craved a road connection to the interior. Repeated appeals to government having failed, the spirited people of the two communities decided to build the road themselves, and commenced the work with such enthusiasm that in a couple of years they had completed the link over terrain that had discouraged government surveyors. The two gangs of amateur road builders, working from each end, met in 1953.

It isn't a high class road though, but it's constantly being improved. At 230 miles from Williams Lake a sign warns that house trailers can proceed no farther on account of steep grades and tight corners. The terrain here rises to the peak elevation of the trip, about 5,000 feet, which is reflected in the keen air and bright alpine flowers which decorate the roadside. Common are arnica, alpine willowherb and large purple fleabane or mountain daisy, while pretty yellow mimulus grows in the occasional small brook which the road crosses.

The easy grades of the plateau are behind now and the country ahead is the kind to tax the ingenuity of professional road builders. One cannot but admire the audacity of the amateurs. "The Hill", as they call it, takes off in a false start down into the canyon of Young Creek, then climbs into the crags again for a fresh swoop into the Bella Coola valley. The abrupt descent of 4,000 feet is accomplished in a series of switch-backs on cliffs and rockslides. There are said to be fine views obtainable from various points of the hill but few motorists notice them. The slowly unfolding track ahead seems to fully engage the attention of driver and passengers alike.

The successful navigation of the hill is not only remarkable for the sense of achievement imparted but also for the astonishing change of scene produced; from the scrub jackpine and spruce of the plateau to the massive and towering pillars of coast timber, the kind of trees that road builders go around. Through the solemn gloom of this forest the road snakes. There are bright glimpses of impatient water scurrying seaward. When the forest thins the snow peaks loom high, cutting off much of the sky, which a short time previously seemed limitless.

Through this wild valley Alexander Mackenzie made his way in 1793 and became the first white man to reach the Pacific coast of British Columbia by land. His route along this last stretch to the sea, unlike Fraser's, is unmarked by highways, railroads, power lines and urban development. Only a narrow, crooked road threads the valley, timidly intruding into a region which has proved unco-operative with men's aspirations. For Bella Coola had its dreams:

"As the two ports of Vancouver and Prince Rupert lie 550 miles apart there would seem to be an obvious need for an intermediate commercial harbour — a need which Bella Coola is well suited to supply. It is the best gateway through the Cascade Range into the Nechaco, Ootsa Lake, and Chilcotin districts, while the Pine River Pass affords better possibilities for a railroad from Bella Coola to Fort St. John ... Immediately behind Bella Coola is an area of 14,000 acres of land eminently adapted by soil and climate to the cultivation of fruit and vegetables ... This town will afford the most satisfactory means of access to the millions of acres in the Peace River district."

So enthused a publication of 1912 when British Columbia was young, and its boosters perhaps a little brash. Mackenzie's valley, in this fifty-mile drive to the sea, is lightly marked by the passage of the years. The few settlers' clearings increase in size as tidewater is approached, and now, inevitably, the loggers are laying down the giant trees. The marks of the springboard loggers are still to be seen in the huge stumps sawn off with "misery whips" twelve or fourteen feet above the ground.

Some of the fertile acres mentioned by the boosters of 1912 are to be seen at Hagensborg, within ten miles of Bella Coola; but it is a miniature settlement that never grew beyond a collection of small farms and homes. Its very smallness gives it a picturesque charm seldom attained by more populous communities. There is a pretty church, apple trees, fields of hay and potatoes, a few grazing cattle, and old log buildings, all set against a wild mountain background, its peaks white with permanent snow standing 9,000 feet above the narrow floor of the valley. Hagensborg was established by settlers of Norwegian origin whose skilful broadaxe work is evident in many of the buildings. A particularly fine example of a hewn log house is to be seen at the Wagon Wheel Cafe. Built in the early days of settlement which date from 1894, the huge squared logs fit so perfectly that the chinking is by way of ornament and serves to delineate the logs. The corners are dovetailed and pinned with wooden dowels, and one gets the impression that the builder intended it to last through the centuries.

During the last few miles of this journey the smell of the sea betrays Bella Coola's maritime state, otherwise the scene, at first glance, could be anywhere in the mountains. The narrow fiord stretches away and is lost behind more mountains just like so many of the interior lakes, but the gulls and the fishing boats, the racks of drying nets, the log rafts sitting on the mud flats awaiting the returning tide are unmistakably coastal.

A far cry, indeed, from the high open flats of Anahim Lake is this quiet, landlocked haven; but the difference was even greater in past times when the Bella Coola native villages bristled with totem poles and house posts, and the cemeteries contained carved grave figures, fascinating relics of a vanished art.

SOME CARIBOO BYWAYS

There was a time when a journey up the Cariboo Road
gave the traveller a sample of the real flavour of that
remarkable country. I recall the early thirties when the
gravel road — washboard all the way — meandered over
the plateau, avoiding large trees and boulders as was the
fashion with the early road builders, swerving over to the
edge of the famous Chasm, where the stage driver always
stopped to give the passengers a look, and continued its
rather aimless way past ranches and road houses where
the traditional hospitality of the Cariboo was
demonstrated in splendid meals for travellers. That, of
course, was in the days of five cent beef.

The crookedness of the original road has been
attributed to either the desire to hunt out the easiest grade
for the freight hauling horses and oxen, or the cunning of
the contractors who stretched out the work to make more
money.

Modern road builders have changed all that and
provided faster, more direct travel, but in so doing they
have destroyed the oldtime atmosphere. Gone are most of
the log road houses, and the famous hostelries too, such as
the Clinton Hotel which was destroyed by fire like most of
the others. Instead of the old log buildings, harmonious
attributes of the Cariboo landscape, brightly painted
service stations and snack bars draw the motorists'
attention while yet a mile away.

But the real Cariboo is still there. Its quieter solitudes
are available to the curious investigator by a network of

side roads distributed over the plateau, and among these, three little roads explore a complete section of the romantic land from its eastern to its western confines. The first starts from Little Fort on the Yellowhead Highway and wanders, like all such country roads, for 63 miles to the Cariboo Highway a few miles south of 100 Mile House. An interesting but imaginative map of British Columbia of 1884 indicates the route follows an old trail, but Little Fort, like Vancouver, was unknown to cartographers at that time, and when it was recognized was first designated Mount Olie. It is a pleasant little settlement in the valley of the North Thompson from which the road ascends into the timber on the west side, to descend again into a deep canyon dark with cedar and devil's club which it follows beside a half-hidden creek, tracing its sinuous course around steep rock bluffs.

Narrow, of course, like all these old roads, with trees growing right to the edge making a dappled pattern of sun and shade so grateful to the summer traveller, it gradually ascends with the creek to finally emerge on the plateau where the open grassland of the ranching country is encountered. But the leisurely wanderer knows the value of frequent halts. There are creek beds to explore. Who knows what desirable rocks are to be found? Rhodonite and a pretty jasper conglomerate are collected in the Barriere River a little to the south, so why not a few miles north? A low road and a slow road is best for the observation of natural productions, plants, birds, and animals, and while squirrels chiefly comprise the last, you may suddenly encounter deer around one of the many sharp bends. The devil's club which grows in this deep bottom is a handsome plant despite its sinister name. It bears a cluster of red berries in the late summer. I once met an Indian in the Skeena country going home with a faggot of the coarse stems of this shrub — going to cure his rheumatism with it, he said.

And the aspen tree is worthy of notice. At plateau level it grows in clumps and is characteristic of the Cariboo. In late September it will be turning gold, some clumps earlier than others, and with the dried grassy hills accentuates the mellow mood of the landscape. In spring the sap layer of this tree can be eaten, being stripped from the wood after the bark has been removed. The native Indians used a bone implement for the purpose, and when travelling this tool and fishing lines were suffficient to secure them sustenance.

The road straggles over the plateau, a country of hills and hollows with many small lakes. Lac des Roches, beside the way, is one of the originals shown on my old map which omits Bridge Lake altogether and has Canim Lake down as Canoe Lake. But Bridge Lake isn't the kind of lake you can ignore. It is about half-way along this road, and has been recognized by summer campers as a desirable place to holiday and fish. On a quiet day it is a little jewel, reflecting the timbered shore in upside-down perfection.

The title, "Fence Viewer", is conferred on persons appointed by municipalities to settle fencing disputes, but you can assume the title yourself when in the Cariboo country for you will certainly see plenty of fences in a number of patterns, in varying states of repair. Everyone will recognize the snake fence of rails or logs but it takes more experience to decide when you have a rare stake and rider in view. A detour around the north side of Bridge Lake will reveal a specimen of this curious pattern. You will go a long way before you find another.

A finer grove of aspens than the group enclosing Bridge Lake government campsite is not to be found on this journey. Much taller than usual, the trees are so old that the bark has become deeply furrowed, almost like that of the cottonwood, with no resemblance to the

An alkali lake tableau ranch horses have a day off.

smooth-skinned saplings on which knife-carrying and unfeeling tourists love to carve their initials.

Continuing westward through jackpines and indifferent ranching country the road skirts the remarkable rock tower of Lone Butte standing solitary like a fortress overlooking the plain. Like the great Chasm farther south, it is a relieving feature in a generally monotonous terrain. Sections through this terrain are occasionally revealed in stream-eroded canyons such as the Chasm and show many layers of lava, the strata lying horizontally. Most of the erratic boulders which are strewn so plentifully over the plateau are obviously derived from this formation. Seven miles past Lone Butte the end of this little country road is proclaimed by the whine of traffic on the Cariboo Highway.

Bridge over Chilcotin River in Farwell Canyon.

To pursue this westward journey across the Cariboo a road leaves the highway ten miles north of Clinton and penetrates as far as the Fraser Canyon near Gang Ranch before swinging north towards Williams Lake for a total distance of 112 miles. The start is over a cattle guard, the ridiculously simple invention that has proved so baffling to horses and cattle, and is now in universal use throughout the ranching country where it replaces the creaking gates of the past. Much of this road is maintained in a primitive state — narrow, very crooked and with some challenging hills in the canyon section to which the few hardy inhabitants are inured. But the first few miles have been improved and lead encouragingly over flat country with small lakes and meadows. At 16 miles, by a cluster of deserted old ranch buildings, a fork and signpost indicate an alternate route to Dog Creek, Alkali Lake and Williams Lake, a more direct one too; but our road, taking the left fork, leads on to Canoe Creek which it follows down into a narrow limestone canyon to emerge at the native village and large ranch of the same name.

We have descended from plateau level into the canyon country, a region of deep gullies and jumbled, arid hills; and the drop in altitude produces a corresponding change of flora. Trees become sparse, growing chiefly in the gullies, and sagebrush takes over much of the terrain, which is also hospitable to rabbit bush, cactus and wormwood. Wherever water can be guided to the silt benches of the canyon bright green squares of alfalfa signify bountiful hay crops; and surely no oasis is a richer green than the long sloping benches of Canoe Creek Ranch set in the arid landscape formed by the gullied flanks of the Fraser Canyon.

This immense landscape, so little known to present day British Columbians, was traversed by the River Trail of 1859 by which the gold miners first travelled to Cariboo. It was quickly supplanted as a route by the

Cariboo Wagon Road which opened a way over the easier terrain of the plateau. Our road today is said to follow this old trail through Dog Creek and Alkali Lake to Springhouse. Dog Creek is reputed to be one of the oldest places of settlement in the interior. It is reached after negotiating the hills previously mentioned which commence rather wildly from a forks near the bottom of the canyon, the left track of which leads to Gang Ranch via the Churn Creek suspension bridge. These are rather alarming hills, both up and down, but so characteristic of the canyon country that the motorist must needs adjust himself rapidly or retire to some gentler terrain for his explorations.

Dog Creek ranch and store sit in a deep hollow in this marvellous landscape, sheltered by steep hills which are crowned, on one side, by the formation known in the Cariboo as the rimrock, those vertical cliffs exposing the several layers of lava that comprise the surface rocks of much of the plateau. It is a quiet spot, certainly less frequented by travellers now than in the old days of horse transport. A report of 1911 mentions the ranch as a stopping place — fully licenced — with stabling for 25 horses; it describes the property as 7,500 acres with 37 miles of fences and 15 miles of irrigation ditch bringing water to 600 acres of crop land. It is claimed that Dog Creek is the site of the first flour mill established on the mainland of the province, a venture of 1866. Later a saw mill was powered by the overshot water-wheel which still sits there, totally concealed from the passer-by though, by a jungle of weeds and shade trees that has overgrown it.

Now 57 miles on our way — about half way — we are still in the canyon country, on a twisting narrow track which ascends ridges and swoops into gullies, offering occasional glimpses of the Fraser from the high spots; a trail like a thread straggling over an immensity of folded, grassy hills. At the right season blooms of the mariposa

This old relic burned down a few years ago. The house of the old-time Meason's ranch near Dog Creek.

lily decorate this arid landscape. Known also as lavender lily, its three-petalled cup waves a foot and-a-half above the parched soil on a leafless stem. Blooming in the hottest and dryest part of the summer this lovely flower has few competitors for attention. Its habitat is restricted to dry and gravelly soils, and in the neighbourhood of Dog Creek its unusual profusion indicates ideal conditions far removed from the greatest threat to its continued existence — people.

For people are very scarce in this lonely land. Fences and cattle-guards tell you it's occupied, but habitations are rarely seen. By a lonely stretch of road a few deserted buildings and a corral denote a former ranch. A big two-story frame house burned down a few years ago. It had an interesting history, for it was once Meason's Ranch, started in 1897 by Captain Wm. Meason, and developed to an 11,000 acre property stretching for 8 miles along the river canyon, with 46 miles of fences. In those days there was good winter range, and feeding of the 700 head of cattle was seldom necessary. Forlorn and deserted now, its land added to the holdings of larger operations, it typifies a story many times repeated throughout the Cariboo and other ranching areas of the interior.

Alkali Lake ranch and native village — 79 miles — the next inhabited place on this road, has an aura of permanence sharply contrasting with dilapidated Meason's. Said to be the first cattle ranch in the Cariboo, started in 1861 on the site of a previous road house on the River Trail which dated from 1859, it grew to be one of the largest and by 1912 is reported to have comprised 25,000 acres with 75 miles of barbed wire fencing and ran 1,500 head of cattle. The native village sits on a bench opposite the ranch, dominated by a church which occupies a place of prominence.

The Alkali Lake settlement shows enough log buildings to preserve the romantic flavour associated with the old Cariboo, but the village itself is changing in appearance with the introduction of modern frame houses and the disappearance of the old grey logs. Satisfaction with the change is not, however, universal. Some of the villagers say the old houses were more comfortable to live in, certainly warmer in winter. They weathered well too, and seemed to grow harmoniously into the landscape like the rocks and the trees; but that is a point on which the Indian inhabitants will offer no opinion.

Fence viewing again keeps the passengers alert, and as the road continues to the Springhouse country, that old

On the Dog Creek-Alkali Lake road. View of the Fraser.

ranchers' standby, the Russell fence, is observed by the
mile on both sides of the road. Photographs of the Cariboo
taken sixty and seventy years ago show the Russell fence.
It has indeed become the hallmark of the cattle country,
especially in the Chilcotin where the raw materials for its
production are more plentiful than in the treeless ranges
of Dog Creek and Alkali Lake. Usually five rails high, with
no posts, the panels being supported by crossed stakes
and the whole being tied securely with thin pliable wire,
the Russell fence appears to be a complicated piece of
work but actually its construction is very simple.

In the Alkali Lake village, 1965.

Now the plateau becomes generally forested, with grassy openings and small lakes; the Fraser Canyon with its bare, flanking hills is away to the west, and fast-growing Williams Lake lies ahead.

We take the Chilcotin Road west from Williams Lake to complete this traverse of the cattle country. About thirty miles out, near Riske Creek, our road turns left to Farwell Canyon and Big Creek. It is a new road without character but it follows an older route which was discontinued after a major landslide in 1964 wiped out part of it and destroyed the bridge over the Chilcotin River. Being new it is wide and unfriendly — deep ditches so you can't pull off just anywhere — but it passes the old familiar scenes, the bald hills and the little native village of Toosey lying in a deep green hollow; and the old track winding like a thin trail over hills and gullies.

It swoops in wide loops down into the incomparable Farwell Canyon of the Chilcotin River and toils up the opposite side in the same manner. It needs an artist to do justice to Farwell Canyon. The photographer cannot hope to reproduce the subtle shades and the purple haze of distance in a photographic print; although he may capture the myriad folds of the eroded hills, the rows of pinnacles sculptured from the sediments of the canyon walls, and the low light of morning or afternoon falling on every prominence. It is an immense, tortured landscape which September softens in mellow shades to a harmonious whole; where the greens are almost absent, and the buffs, browns, fawns and russets, and the indefinable tints of the sparse, burnt-up herbage blend with the exposed silts and gravels of the canyon walls.

Intruding into this sober scene the exquisite turquoise water of the river flashes in startling glimpses where the channel is occasionally revealed between the cliffs far below.

The great scar of the 1964 landslide, now a sheer cliff in a thick silt deposit, shows where the canyon wall collapsed, completely blocking the river and backing up the water until it drowned the old bridge which was later swept away in the rush of water when the river broke through the obstruction. Only the piers remain.

Several bands of Shuswap Indians once occupied the canyon but they were practically wiped out by smallpox in 1862 and the few survivors joined other bands. Known among the natives as the "people of the canyon" they had villages on both sides of the river. They left some traces in the form of pictographs which are to be seen on an overhanging rock on a small bench a short distance from the far side of the new bridge.

Climbing the long hill the huge canyon is seen from the other side and from a greater height when the plateau is attained. The character of the country changes as we enter the jackpine-shrouded territory of the Big Creekers, those hardy denizens of the woods who sought and found seclusion in the remote meadows that lie in the high country between the Chilcotin River and the Coast Range. Chiefly forested, the monotony of the scenery is relieved here and there by small meadows, and open grassy flats frequented by the brilliant mountain bluebird which seems to be as much at home in the solitudes as in the domestic surroundings of farm and village.

Thirty-seven miles from Riske Creek we reach the end of our journey. It seems a strange place to select for a destination, and brings to mind the words of R.L. Stevenson: "To travel hopefully is a better thing than to arrive." Big Creek, in fact, would seem to be a more suitable place for departure. But it has its attractions for the pioneering types who have occupied these high meadows since 1903. The post office is located at the Church Ranch which is still in the hands of the original family. The pioneer H.E. Church related his early experiences at Big Creek in a book *An Emigrant in the Canadian North-West,* which is long out of print. In his time, when horses were the means of transportation, Big Creek was indeed remote. In 1904 it took Church, his wife and young family, six days to travel in to their pre-emption from Ashcroft, the nearest rail point.

THE WAYSIDE FENCES

Roads and fences are often close companions. Together they weave distinctive and curious patterns over many landscapes, frequently adding interesting and picturesque features to the natural scene. This is particularly evident in interior British Columbia where the abundance of natural fencing material ensures a rustic boundary to many of our country roads. The fences themselves are an interesting study. To the student of history they speak of times past and the changing pace of life. Consider the snake rail fence built of split rails, lichen-covered and sagging but still serving its purpose after half a century of weathering. It is a relic of more leisurely days. Nobody splits rails any more, so the presence of this material in a fence almost certainly brands it a pioneer job or one rebuilt from pioneer material.

It brings to mind men working in the winter bush cutting and splitting rails; teams hauling loaded sleighs; small snow-covered clearings in the woods; log houses, sheds and barns; coal-oil lamps and the smoke of wood-burning stoves; sleigh bells and the merry, bouncing jingle from the more speedy cutters; and the wheezing and rasping of hand-cranked gramophones in dimly lighted rooms. To many people rail fences and pioneer days are synonymous. In Ontario old hand split rails from the pioneers' fences are sought by urban residents for landscaping purposes and garden decorations. British Columbians haven't reached that stage yet — there are too many of the old fences still around for them to be regarded in the light of antiques. In fact their utility still endears

them to farmers and ranchers who find them more economical to maintain than wire fence.

Observant travellers will notice many different patterns in rail fences — and there is a reason for every pattern, generally more substantial then the mere whim of the builder. There are farmers' fences and ranchers' fences, each in its own particular style adapted to the conditions of the locality; there are post-and-rail fences, A fences, snake fences, and the ingeniously contrived Russell fence which decorates so much of the Cariboo country. The post-and-rail is essentially a farmers' fence and may be seen in the moister interior valleys where agriculture is the important occupation. Agricultural soils are favourable to the digging of post holes, an activity that doesn't appeal too much to ranchers. The farmer has succulent crops to protect, so his rails are laid close together, thus frustrating the dairy cow whose preference for the forage on the other side of the fence is well known.

The well built post-and-rail fence represents a lot of labour but it is durable and can be rebuilt when the inevitable decay of the posts renders this necessary. To the settler it was a most economical fence; the materials cost him nothing and were obtained in the process of clearing land, so his labour was very well applied. The original and most popular method of attaching the rails to the posts was by means of a stake set a few inches from the post, forming a slot into which the rails were inserted, the whole held together by several bands of wire around post and stake.

Country roads and side roads yield the best results for fence collectors, the highways having long ago encroached on the roadside relics of former days. I remember an ancient log fence that bordered the Trans-Canada Highway near Ashcroft Manor in the Thompson Valley. It was a real pioneer relic built of big fir logs, three high, and had reached that wonderful state of decay where every log showed the fascinating texture of extreme weathering which was further enhanced by brightly coloured lichens. It rambled for miles alongside the old road, still serviceable despite its years, and certainly more becoming to the Thompson landscape than the wire which later replaced it. For the old log fence interfered with highway improvement and is no longer to be seen. Other log fences, equally old, still grace the landscape in many parts of the interior, some of them, alas, marking the scene of some industrious settler's attempt to establish ranch and home in the face of low precipitation and lack of water. Westwold, which started its ranching history as Grande Prairie, still retains a number of these fine old relics; and in the Lillooet country mouldering remains snake across the dry, canyon benches and sagebrush flats. A century old, these canyon fences, together with a few roofless and rotting log buildings, and the faint lines of abandoned irrigation ditches, are the only evidence remaining that green fields existed long ago in the everlasting sagebrush. In the Cariboo and Chilcotin districts the log fence has had a flourishing history and is still a familiar feature of the landscape.

There was a time when the building of log fences languished. The labour involved in their construction rendered them too expensive in a period of rising costs. But the mechanical revolution which introduced the pickup baler and depopulated the ranch bunk-houses also brought the chain saw. The tobacco-chewing ranch hands departed along with the horses; the pitchfork became obsolete, so did the crosscut saw which the pioneers relied on; but the few mechanics who remained on the ranch could cut more logs with the new weapon than a whole crew toiling with the "misery whips" of former days.

The new log fences to be seen in the ranching country today are evidence of the productivity of the chain saw, and also of the inherent quality of the fence which has

Snake fence of Jackpine logs in Chilcotin country.

been recognized by ranchers since earliest times. A well set up log fence will outlast all others and can be maintained indefinitely by the occasional replacement of the top log. Its sturdiness renders it the most effective barrier to stock, which is the reason why the use of logs in corral construction is almost universal in the cattle country. Naturally most plentiful in forested country, log fences are also to be seen snaking across the treeless landscape of the Douglas Lake Ranch in the Nicola country. They are encountered along many Cariboo side roads in the well known zigzag pattern from which is derived the designation snake fence. But some ranchers, probably with more time to devote to the work, build a log fence that doesn't zig-zag. The logs are laid straight along, and the ends of the panels connected by short blocks which are notched and fitted to the logs after the fashion of log buildings. A fine example of this type borders a road in Turtle Valley which is reached by a short detour off the Trans-Canada near Chase. This particular fence is a product of more leisurely days and is sufficiently aged to have become a harmonious feature of the landscape, just as authentic as the rocks and the trees.

There is more variety of pattern to be found in rail fences, for the kind erected is almost certainly governed by local conditions, the type of ground and availability of materials being the chief considerations. Rocky ground discourages the digging of post holes so other means of supporting the rails are adopted. The most primitive, of course, is the snake fence where the rails are simply laid on the ground zig-zag fashion and built up to the required height. It was much in vogue in early days on outlying bush farms and even today is commonly found by following country roads in the interior of the province. The Chilcotin country seems to be the natural home of the log fence, being unusually well supplied with the raw material in its extensive jackpine forests, aptly named "the sticks"; but it is probable that the type of cattle raised there has something to do with the question. These animals — "critters", I believe, is the correct term — despise wire fences, but are willing to accept rails or logs except in intolerable circumstances.

So the rail fence is characteristic of the Chilcotin landscape, and, like the old log buildings, has come to be regarded as a natural attribute of the scenery. Most patterns are to be found there but the Russell fence appears to be the favourite at the present time, probably on account of its sparing use of materials. It requires only five rails to a panel, crossed stakes instead of posts, and is built in a straight line, thus needing much less material than the meandering snake fence. A Russell fence and a couple of cowpunchers thrown in are all the ingredients

The rare stake-and-rider fence flourishes in the Anahim district of Chilcotin.

required if the photographer would capture the true flavour of the Chilcotin.

Something in the way of an anomoly and certainly the least common of all the rail fences is the stake-and-rider. Defying the rule of the horizontal governing every other rail fence, the stake-and-rider's bristly appearance derives from the unique pattern formed by the sloping rails. I can recall seeing this type in only four places in the interior. The first was at Big Creek many years ago where I built the thing myself, following the instructions of the rancher for whom I was working. Much later I ran into another specimen near Bear Creek in the vicinity of Chase, and a further discovery at Bridge Lake in the Cariboo convinced me that the type was not a mere freak of one man's fancy. The fourth location of this curious fence is Anahim Lake in the remote Chilcotin, where the scope of the work astonished me. The long stretches of stake-and rider standing here indicate an unusual interest and confidence in the design. I used to think of the stake-and-rider as a makeshift or temporary fence but the Anahim Lake examples are clearly intended to be permanent, and to this end carry reinforcements which are not attempted in less pretentious jobs.

The principle of the stake-and-rider is mutual support, the stakes supporting the riders (rails) and the riders holding down the stakes. The work is commenced by securing one end of a rail to a post or tree at the desired height of the fence — say five feet — and letting the rail slope to the ground where it forms an angle of about thirty degrees. Across this rail, about four feet from the upper end, are driven two stakes which form a crotch into which the next rail is laid, sloping to the ground and lying parallel to the first. This simple procedure is repeated until the required length of fence is standing and the unusual pattern established.

After viewing a stake-and-rider, a fence collector can muster little enthusiasm for barbed wire which is, of course, commonplace in all farming and ranching areas, and is regarded as detrimental to the scenery, like hydro and telephone wires. It borders many miles of roads in the same monotonous pattern of posts and wires, with an occasional variation in the shape of interwoven stakes to add to its effectiveness. But one rancher in the rock-covered open spaces of Upper Hat Creek has discovered an interesting alternative to digging post holes in that hostile ground. Instead of posts he devised tripods made with stakes and fitted with a platform six inches above the ground, on which he piled rocks — of which there is an oversupply on his land — to the weight of several hundred pounds. These sturdy pylons served as posts in supporting several tight strands of barbed wire, stapled in the usual manner. This type of fence covers considerable ground at Upper Hat Creek, its usefulness as a barrier amply demonstrated by its age and the fact that some of the pylons had been recently repaired. Obviously, the rancher was satisfied with his fence and continued to maintain it.

I mentioned this curious fence to my friend, Mrs. Adler, of Little Kingdom Ranch, Six-mile Creek. She remembered the fence from her ranching experiences at Upper Hat Creek many years ago, but couldn't name it. She laughed about the rocks. "Fencing was always a problem there," she said; "it's really a rugged country." Actually, this pylon-wire fence is a demonstration of the resourcefulness of ranchers in making the best use of local material — even though the most plentiful material is rock.

DRY-BELT RIVER

One of the most interesting rivers in British Columbia, I think, is the principal tributary of the Fraser, the Thompson, which occupies a valley notable for its wild scenery and the ruggedness of its canyons. Named for David Thompson, who, it is said, never saw the river himself, it drains a large area between the Columbia and the Fraser, drawing most of its water from the snowy mountains which lie beyond the dry-belt, and conducting it through that region in a tantalizing channel generally too deep and inaccessible to do the parched bench lands any good. The river is like a blue ribbon bisecting the sun-baked landscape of sober colours and eroded formations. It teases the ranchers on the high, valley benches who cannot grow crops without irrigation water. It passes unattainable through a thirsty land.

But perhaps the scenery of the Thompson Valley is all the better because of this aridness which inhibits the spread of greenery so familiar in other parts of the province. Certainly the character of the dry country is more open; the folds and contours of the hills not buried and hidden under dense forest but sparsely dotted with solitary western pines generally quite evenly spaced. The rock colours predominate, and the greens, when they do occur, are all the more attractive because of their scarcity. Cottonwoods by the river in bright spring foliage, irrigated fields and benches so far apart that they may be described as oases, represent the few splashes of bright green that this dry country has to offer.

Cattle coming down from range, Deadman Valley, Thompson country.

These conditions are particularly relevant to that half of the valley which lies between the mouth of the river at Lytton, and Savona where the river, emerging from Kamloops Lake, drops into the picturesque canyon which has caused so much trouble to road and railroad builders since 1862, when the first attempt to establish a route to the interior through it was made. The passage was accomplished first by rough and narrow wagon road and ferry, then, a quarter of a century later, by the C.P.R. and subsequently by the C.N.R. which executed amazing feats on what was at first considered the inaccessible side of the canyon. The building of these three lines of communication and the more recent development of the Trans-Canada Highway on the track of the old wagon road seems to have used up all useful space in the canyon, leaving indeed little enough for the river itself which in places has to be confined by extensive cribbing.

More rugged and picturesque than the lower Fraser Canyon which is now disfigured by the wide swaths of Hydro's transmission lines, the Thompson Canyon, while permitting a flow of traffic, still retains its primitive aspect. Actually, the twisting threads of highway and railroads dwarfed by the high and rocky walls emphasize the grandeur of the scenery. Between Lytton and Spences Bridge signs of established settlement are confined to a few tiny benches in which fruit trees, including apricot and peach, indicate a climate less hostile than the terrain. Here and there, too, hillsides less than precipitous are grazed by a few sure-footed cattle whose natural inclination to follow the horizontal corrugations or terraces in such hillsides has fostered the widely held belief that such terracing is artificially produced. Geologists say that the phenomenon of terracing on steep hillsides is due to a natural process known as slumping or soil creep, and this view is supported by the observations of an early traveller in the Thompson Canyon, Dr.

Cheadle, who traversed the partly-built wagon road in 1863. He noted and described the terraced hillsides before cattle ranching had become established in the interior.

One modification of the Thompson landscape which can be attributed to ranching is the replacement of the original bunch grass by sagebrush, which has degraded much of the interior range land. Demonstrations of this transition may be seen in the canyon where the right-of-way of the C.P.R. is fenced across some of these hillsides. Inside the fence the protected hillsides are rich with luxuriant bunch grass, while the adjoining overgrazed range supports little but sagebrush. Old maps of the interior designate much of the Thompson Valley's sagebrush-covered land "undulating bunch grass country."

Shaw Springs, in the bottom of the canyon 16 miles from Lytton, was a stop-over place in the days when the primitive state of the canyon road rendered the journey from coast to interior a two-day affair. Many travellers remember the hospitality of Bill Shaw and his late and very much lamented sister Leah. Bill once took me rock hunting in his four-wheel-drive vehicle, climbing out of the canyon up a crazy logging road and then taking off across country on the plateau. I was badly frightened on this trip but recovered enough to collect a quantity of agate nodules which are quite plentiful there. Coast rockhounds heading into the interior where the agates are to be found know Shaw Springs as a good collecting area, and are encouraged to continue and explore the extensive volcanic outcrops farther up the valley. These rocks are well exposed on account of the scanty vegetation of the region, and are thus easily prospected. They yield a variety of interesting and desirable stones.

At Spences Bridge, where the route crosses the river, the original crossing for the early wagon road traffic was by ferry, and the place was known as Cook's Ferry after the man who supplied the connection. Cook, however, became a victim to advancing technology as practised by a Mr. Spence who built a bridge and thus deprived his predecessor of his rightful place in posterity. Travellers over this route in the eighteen-sixties remarked on the ruggedness of the terrain, the difficulties of the road and the constant work being done to improve it. It was then, as it is today, the chief route to Cariboo, and must have presented to those early travellers essentially the same scenes the modern motorist observes. The old wagon road was narrow and in places bordered by log fences which endured until the fairly recent upgrading to highway standards swept all such relics away. But across the river — safe from the highway engineer — some relics endure, enhancing the old-time atmosphere of the valley. Little old log buildings and straggling fences mark the deserted native village of Pokhaist with its small church posed against an overpowering background of rockslide and mountain.

In this area, between Spences Bridge and Ashcroft, settlement scarcely touched the valley until modern irrigation equipment began to deliver water to previously dry benches. A century of ranching passed with little effect on the natural scene. The country is just too dry and the creeks coming from the mountains too few to make possible extensive irrigation. But the little tracks that take off here and there up into the hills lead to enterprises, mostly small, where some sheltered meadow and convenient open range suggested possibilities to the pioneers. Not all of these small ranches survived, and there are enough relics of decaying log houses and barns, and stretches of old barbed wire of a pattern long out of fashion to indicate that the optimism of the early ranchers was not always justified. Sometimes when following these rough side roads one encounters earthworks of considerable size in the form of dams and ditches obviously intended for the diversion of water for irrigation purposes. Examples are to be seen at Upper Hat Creek which can be reached by taking the narrow but interesting road up the valley of Oregon Jack Creek which joins the highway some distance west of Ashcroft Manor; and in the remote highlands of Botanie Valley near Lytton. Both these examples are impressive works representing the excavation of enormous quantities of soil. They can safely be assigned to the shovel and horsescraper period of the late nineteenth centurey; in fact, one rancher told me these works were produced by gangs of Chinese labourers inured to the use of the shovel. This labour pool became available to the ranchers on the completion of the C.P.R. which employed them in building the grade, and would date these earthworks at 1866 or a bit later.

Fifteen miles upriver from Spences Bridge a little road turns off the highway to Venables Valley, a minor feature of the Thompson country scarcely warranting a name, but it contains several curious lakes heavily charged with mineral substances including epsomite which was mined there at one time. Various stages of evaporation produce circular patterns on the surface of the lakes, with rich and unusual colour effects sure to interest those who are intrigued by natural curiosities. Although the water is undrinkable and poisonous to livestock the small lakes fit harmoniously into a pine-studded landscape well granished with exposures of bare rock. They are fenced against the hardy cattle that graze, and thrive, on the scanty range.

Forty-six miles from the mouth of the Thompson the little town of Ashcroft sits in the arid valley bottom at what was originally a strategic point in the interior. Born of the railway, Ashcroft immediately became the supply and shipping point for the settled country served by the

The Thompson River near Walhachin flows through a dry valley of sagebrush flats and naked hills.

Cariboo Road. This extended north as far as Barkerville, the focal point of the gold mining activity that preceded the rapid settlement of the interior of the province. The Thompson Valley superseded the Lillooet route which had proved a toilsome and roundabout way to the Cariboo gold creeks, and when the railway penetrated the valley Ashcroft became the new and more convenient terminal of the Cariboo Road. This remarkable road originally started at Yale, the head of river navigation in the lower Fraser Canyon, but the canyon section was rendered obsolete at the time by the building of the C.P.R. which followed the same route. A brief description of the shortened road as it was in the mid eighteen-eighties is contained in a letter from a Cariboo miner to a friend in Vancouver instructing him how to get to the gold fields. The letter was dated at

Stanley, a town that has completely disappeared, and reads, in part, as follows:

" . . . to come to Cariboo you come with the C.P.R. as far as Ashcroft. The stage comes to Ashcroft but they charge so much if you are not in a hurry I would walk it. It is about 300 miles there is plenty of places on the road to stop if a man is not in a hurry it is the best. It takes 5 days from Ashcroft to Barkerville in fine weather with the stage and I am 14 miles from Barkerville. They will charge you between 40 and 50 dollars and they will pack two pairs of blankets. But the difference in price up here is not much if you bring just what you have got it will be enough. There is nothing but miners right here but down 70 miles there is quite a few farms. It is too cold here for farming there is farms here and there all the way down to Ashcroft but the farming is on a small scale . . ."

The arid character of the Thompson Valley is nowhere more apparent than in the vicinity of Ashcroft, where the valley trends easterly in an almost treeless landscape towards the bare hills enclosing Kamloops Lake. The scene today is desert-like, with wide flats and benches supporting little but sagebrush and cactus, between flanking hills of bare, red rock; but many years ago an ambitious irrigation project transformed a section of the dry valley, creating an oasis of orchards and vegetable fields. The short-lived settlement of Walhachin has been the subject of many stories and is commemorated today by a sign beside the highway between Cache Creek and Savona. "Ghost of Walhachin," the sign says, very appropriately, for you can still see a few thorny-looking apple trees sticking up here and there amongst the sage.

This scheme for making the desert bloom originated in 1907 through the enterprise of Mr. C.E. Barnes who acquired over 3,000 acres, portioned it into 10 acre tracts and commenced planting fruit trees. By 1911 Walhachin was a settlement of 200 people, mostly immigrants from the United Kingdom, and photographs of the period show healthy young orchards interplanted with potatoes. Water was brought 20 miles by a flume which tapped Deadman River, but when the flume was partly destroyed by one of the heavy cloudbursts that occasionally hit the dry-belt the promotors were unable to gather the resources to make repairs, and the orchards soon went back to the desert. Remnants of the flume are still to be seen clinging to the rocky bluffs of the dry valley. Some old-timers ranching in the district say that Walhachin was doomed to failure anyway as Deadman River was not an adequate source of water for such a large irrigation project.

Deadman Valley itself trends north from the highway through a parched country of many-coloured volcanic rocks, the small river in its centre making itself known by a few crooked cottonwoods along its course. The colourful rocks of this section of the Thompson Valley extend past Savona and along the north shore of Kamloops Lake, providing that body of water with an unusually interesting setting. The reds and yellows in the vicinity of Copper Creek, reflected in periods of calm, the huge bold outline of Battle Bluff, and the gullied and serrated hills between these two features, present the true dry-belt landscape where land and water, so strictly segregated, fail to generate that explosion of greenery that surrounds so many of our British Columbia lakes. Is it this naked aspect that has caused Kamloops Lake to remain unsung while Shuswap and Okanagan have long inspired local poets and Chambers of Commerce? Perhaps its barren beauty would have been more esteemed if it had been accessible, but to the traveller it has always been remote, its tantalizing water far below the highway, unattainable as a mirage on a hot summer day.

There was a time when the pure air of the dry-belt was considered beneficial to people with weak lungs, and a sanatorium for their treatment was maintained for many

The rock pillars of Deadman Valley.

The white silt formation of South Thompson Valley, east of Kamloops.

years at Tranquille near the east end of the lake; but now the haze from industrial Kamloops somewhat clouds the scene, introducing the odours of pulp mill and refinery into the realm of pine and juniper and sage. Happily the character of the terrain resists urbanization which is chiefly concentrated in Kamloops, a rather surprising city in a comparatively empty land. Kamloops has always been a crossroads, a place to stop after long journeys. From there you can go north, south, east or west over long-established routes provided by the valleys which converge there. Archaeological remains indicate a considerable native population on the site of Kamloops before the fur traders came and built their post on what was an empty flat where the North and South Thompson rivers came together.

In those days the river was the life of the valley, bringing sustenance to the native inhabitants, and the banks were pitted with the winter homes of the Shuswap who took full advantage of the annual salmon spawning run. It must have been a pleasant place to live — waterfront homes with no taxes — along a quiet stream so different from the turbulent lower reaches, and each summer and fall the runs of salmon to provide a season of easy living. The salmon still come and are now regarded in the light of a tourist attraction, drawing annually many visitors to the valley.

From Kamloops, where the river forks, this South Thompson is a lazy stream, gliding between banks lined with willow and cottonwood and aspen, bordered by castellated white silt cliffs, and home to beaver colonies that carry out their tree-felling activities within sight of city lights. Once the route of early steamboats that navigated the reaches of Shuswap Lake and Shuswap River it now provides a convenient waterway for Kamloops boat owners who go that way to reach those delectable waters. The green and forested hills of Shuswap proclaim the limits of the dry-belt, and also the source of the South Thompson in Little Shuswap Lake.

BACK ROAD TO LILLOOET

Of all the little towns in the interior, Lillooet has always been my favourite because of the beauty of its setting and its romantic historical associations. It lies in a particularly rugged section of the Fraser Canyon at a point where a narrow gap opens a way through the mountains to the Pacific coast. Through this pass came the first stream of traffic from the settlements on the coast, adventurers from many lands heading for the interior where the bars of the Fraser and the creeks of Cariboo promised riches in the form of newly-discovered placer gold. The scenery is mountainous and tends to the vertical in tremendous exposures of unclothed rock reaching up to snowy summits; and the bench on which the little town sits is a wide expansion of the Fraser Canyon generously supplied by nature as if for the purpose of a settlement.

Lillooet has breathing room in the canyon, the river valley opening to the south a hazy vista of receding ridges blue with distance, but behind the town a majestic wall of mountains blocks out the northern sky. The nature of this terrain decrees that all roads in the vicinity are exciting and interesting to drive on, but unfortunately this precipitous quality has resulted in much modern disfigurement by Hydro transmission lines which converge in the vicinity, swooping in enormous shining leaps from mountain-top to mountain-top. The price of progress is heavy indeed in this magnificent mountain area.

Lillooet was only a moderate drive from our farm — about 160 miles — and on the frequent occasions when our work permitted it we drove to the old town to make it a headquarters for trips of exploration in its fascinating surroundings. "Back Road to Lillooet" deals with the tenuous western outlet to Vancouver which the local people hope will be eventually developed into a practical route.

It isn't an instant road, like the Rogers Pass section or the Nelson-Creston highway, built and finished completely with paving and white line. The back road to Lillooet is an example of slow evolution, the joining of several links in which the sections of rough track eventually become a route. But in this case the process has not advanced to the stage where the term "road", as understood by motorists, can be applied to every one of its crooked miles.

Lillooet saw the very start of interior road-building, for in 1861 a wagon road towards Cariboo was commenced from a point on the Fraser opposite the town, which was at that time an important and bustling stopping-place on the trail to the new gold discoveries. This early road which climbed steeply out of the canyon was an improvement to the Douglas Route by which the first miners reached the Cariboo creeks, a roundabout tour involving the passage of several lakes and the intervening portages and trails. Lillooet was not accessible by continuous road until the opening of the Cariboo Road up the Fraser Canyon, and even then it was by-passed by the main route which was diverted through the Thompson Canyon more than forty miles away. It became a town with no back door, a condition that the coming of the P.G.E. in 1916 relieved occasionally by a mixed train to Squamish.

It is now possible for those of adventurous spirit and vehicles not too lowly slung to drive to Lillooet by the back road which follows, in part, the route of the railway. Vancouverites cross Second Narrows Bridge and continue through North and West Vancouver and along the rocky

Bridge over Deep Gorge-D'Arcy-Seton Portage mountain road.

Dogwood blooms in the bush near Mount Currie.

and arbutus-clad cliffs of Howe Sound to Squamish where the route turns inland up a valley which used to be the exclusive territory of the P.G.E. [Now the British Columbia Railway.] When that interesting railroad's terminal was at Squamish passengers and freight would come by water from Vancouver and embark on the mixed train, to proceed hopefully in the direction of Quesnel. In those days in summer the antique passenger cars and perhaps an observation car would be crowded with happy holiday-makers bound for the little resorts along the route between Squamish and Lillooet.

The P.G.E. has been abused and ridiculed but it opened up a country of outstanding scenic beauty, a region of small lakes and steep mountains that could not be conveniently reached by other means, and if its trains were slow and uncertain they were regarded with affection by railroad enthusiasts who came from all over North America to ride in the antiquated cars. These queer conveyances were salvaged, it is said, from the scrap heaps of more prosperous lines. I remember the ornate fittings, the big brass lamps swinging from the ceiling, and the comfortless seats, when travelling the route in the nineteen-thirties.

The railroad pioneered the way; the road followed gradually, and then the little resorts no longer depended on the P.G.E. to bring their guests. From Squamish the road skirts Garibaldi Park to Alta Lake and thence to Pemberton, that previously remote settlement where farmers used their isolation to advantage by developing a profitable business in seed potatoes. Near Pemberton the original Douglas Route came in from the south via Harrison and Lillooet lakes. It seems strange now to think that traffic to the interior used this tortuous way, but until the Fraser Canyon was opened up there was no better route.

The travellers, Milton and Cheadle, went from New Westminster to Barkerville by this route in 1863. Their journey was made out of curiosity as they were already familiar with the new and speedier Fraser Canyon road, and their observations included scenery, for which the miners, frustrated by the many impediments to travel, expressed little regard. "The scenery on this route," they wrote, "especially on the lakes Anderson and Seton, is exceedingly wild and grand. Mountains rise sharply from the shores of the lakes on each side, steep, rugged, and barren; and when we saw them their beauty was increased by the brilliant tints of the American autumn."

Milton and Cheadle viewed these scenes from the decks of steamboats, a pleasure no longer to be had as the route of the lakes has been long abandoned. Now the railroad skirts one shore and the other is too precipitous to offer footing for a road. From Pemberton to D'Arcy at the

124

beginning of Anderson Lake the road dwindles. Actually this is the end of normal road travel. The country ahead is extremely rugged, as it is through all the Lillooet country, and the roads that are built or scratched through it are not ordinary roads. D'Arcy is a quaint village with a little white Indian church and a cemetery well packed with headstones and markers which hint that life in this quiet valley is conducive to longevity. One, Joseph Joe, is credited with attaining 119 years, a life which spans all the history of the white man in these parts.

There are old apple trees and very old log buildings, a combination characteristic of the native villages in this valley of the narrow lakes. Across the creek the artificial spawning beds for salmon strike a modern note with the geometrically precise grid of shallow ditches. The road to Lillooet can be found by hunting around the buildings until you strike the trail that crosses the railroad. It leads very steeply up the mountain and doesn't level off until the valley lies below like a map. Anderson Lake appears as a long, narrow trough skirted by the P.G.E. track which follows the contour of the shore. Snow mountains notch the horizon.

This particular stretch of road follows B.C. Hydro's transmission lines for 17 miles along the whole length of Anderson Lake. These too-obvious signs of progress do nothing to improve the scenery. Wide swaths cleared along the mountainside, steel towers and the soaring loops between, frustrate the photographer impressed by the natural beauty of the scene; but it is possible on occasion to avoid the wires and record a landscape primitive and wild. Without the towers and wires there would, of course, be no road, and the few shy prospectors who inhabit the mountains would be better pleased. About half a dozen miles from D'Arcy one of these hermits lived in quiet seclusion until Hydro's crews rudely disturbed her wilderness. This lady prospector's flumes are seen beside the road and there is a gate cross to keep her horses from straying.

A track leads off into the bush, and following it the curious traveller comes to an old log cabin with shake roof, other small buildings, a woodpile, and flumes leading here and there. There's likely to be a notice on the door: "Gone to your place," — a sure indication of another hermit in the neighbourhood. Leona Weeden is nearly 80 years old and still spends her summers on the mountain where she works some bench leases with water flumed from McGillivray Creek. Part of her ground, she says, is on a former channel of the creek, and that's where the values are, but she frequently has to move big boulders to get at the pay dirt. A placer mining company formerly worked the creek but Mrs. Weeden has it to herself now, having held ground there since '33. Lumber for her flumes and sluices was brought up the mountain on pack-horses from the railroad 800 feet below, for previous to the road the only access to this country was by trail. "You can't beat this life," she says, with authority, having spent many years trapping and prospecting. But the road's got her worried. "Getting too darned civilized around here," she complains. "Cars passing nearly every day."

Another track leads higher still on the mountain, where McGillivray Creek cuts a deep canyon, to the old Anderson Lake Mine, staked in the early days and equipped with a ten stamp mill which was freighted up the mountain on pack horses. The old mill was replaced by a more up-to-date plant dating from the Bridge River boom days of the nineteen-thirties, and this gaunt and deserted building rears high on the mountain, solitary in a sea of peaks.

Like most of the prospects of those days this old mine never did prove a profitable operation. I knew it when the old-time prospector, Charlie Noel, optioned the property and broke out some spectacular free gold ore, but the

D'Arcy church and cemetery at the foot of the mountain road to Lillooet.

values proved spotty, and the abandoned mill now stands as a monument to unrealized hopes.

As the track continues the terrain gets rougher. Even for the Lillooet country this Seton-D'Arcy 17-mile stretch is an unusual road. It takes you to the heights, leads you gingerly around precipices and along the edges of vertical drops; it crosses a deep gorge on a high, slender, wooden bridge. It is a roller-coaster road designed for sloth instead of speed. From the road's edge you can look down — straight down — any maybe see a train, incredibly far below, worming its slow and sinuous way along the lake's edge. There, but for the P.G.E., would go the road.

In summer these tremendous views are framed through the foamy blooms of scented flowering shrubs, glimpsed over purple patches of sun-loving penstemon, or under the crooked limbs of rock-dwarfed pines — exquisite scenes impressed on passengers with wildly palpitating hearts.

Coming from Lillooet this 17-mile stretch is supposed to be more difficult. The first hill used to be the chief obstacle on the route, according to the locals who were known to say that if you could overcome it you could get through. However, this maxim no longer holds good, for recent work on the hill has reduced the grade and rendered it less difficult. I passed a motorist who had fallen into the trap. Having successfully navigated the first hill he was stuck at the bottom of a steeper one which his vehicle had vainly tried to conquer. He sheepishly admitted he'd been there all night, having sent his wife hiking off for help.

Getting down to Seton Portage is accomplished quite slowly, crawling down the steep hill with several hairpin bends so tight that you have to manoeuvre to make the turns. A story that a local man had driven a two-ton truck with a load of hay over this stretch would have been discredited if the evidence — bales of hay fallen from the load — had not been observed along the road.

There is little evidence now to indicate that the Cariboo traffic of 1860 streamed through this deep and narrow valley, steamboated the lengths of the lakes in the sternwheelers *Champion* and *Lady of the Lake,* and crossed the 1½ mile isthmus of Seton Portage by way of a wooden railway. Some traces of the railway remain where the narrow grade was built up on low ground. Mrs. J.A. Edwards who keeps a resort at Seton can point out a section where it crosses her property. The other antiquities of the place are the buildings. Surely these ancient logs date from those early times! You glimpse them in the native villages nearly hidden behind gnarled apple and apricot trees; and a tiny abandoned church too, raises its diminutive spire out of a mass of chokecherry.

The quiet torpor of this idyllic spot, interrupted by a rush of miners 110 years ago, is now disturbed periodically by the harsh mechanical vibrations of the P.G.E. whose long freights pass through daily.

Now at the head of Seton Lake we are only 20 miles, by water, from Lillooet — a route naturally favoured by the local crows — but there is no room in that deep trench for a road. Our route has to climb, and there are 45 miles of mountain road between us and our destination. The way leads through Bridge River townsite and plant, a web of steel — transformers, transmission towers and lines striking through the scenery; gigantic penstocks drooping down the mountain like lethargic, uncoiled, black snakes. Ever since it was discovered that Bridge River, flowing just behind the mountain, was 1,200 feet higher than Seton Lake, engineers have been planning and developing; and the diverted river now flows through tunnels in the mountain to take its plunge unseen to the power-houses on Seton Lake.

The road goes over the mountain, to descend into the Bridge River valley and follow it to Lillooet. It is a steady climb of 3,000 feet to the top of the ridge. At the base of this hill just out of sight of the wilderness of steel of the power plant is the Indian village of Shalalth where the narrow spire of the Roman Catholic church supports a white cross high over the tranquil lake.

This mountain road has changed little since its beginning when it was the only route into the Bridge River gold mines, and the access to the B.C. Electric dam and tunnel sites in the valley. Until quite recently the old Company signs could still be seen here and there on the hill. These warned drivers: "Any employee of the company caught exceeding 15 miles per hour on this road will be instantly fired." I was directed over this road by an old prospector in Lillooet in the early thirties when I was heading for the upper Bridge with saddle and pack horses.

I remember his directions: "You'll have to ride the track along Seton Lake, Son. We used to have a trail but the P.G.E. wrecked it. Let's see — there's no train today — only two trains a week anyway. You take to the track at Craig Lodge and keep a' going, but don't try to cross the trestles — there's two of them but a bit of a trail detours them. It heads right up the mountain but don't get discouraged — it climbs down again in time. When you get to Shalalth there's a road goes up over the mountain and down into the Bridge River valley."

This road saw much traffic during the Bridge River gold boom of the thirties. There was no connection with Lillooet at that time and all freight to the mines came in on the P.G.E. and was trucked over the mountain. In the peak year of the boom over 4,000 claims were recorded and nearly 1,200 certificates of work issued, something of a record for any mining district at that time; and ten thousand tons of freight moved over the mountain for the forty companies working in the valley.

From the higher twists of this road the lakes Anderson and Seton appear as two narrow turquoise pools forming the very bottom of a vertical landscape that is crowned by snow peaks floating high in the hazy atmosphere — delicate, distant peaks, seeming intangible compared with the ruddy pine trunks that frame the view. This is Lillooet scenery at its best. The descent on the Bridge River side presents a different scene — a drowned valley where for years the skeletons of trees stood in the water. Some of them have floated up now and are gathered in rafts of driftwood. Carpenter Lake, created by a dam which cut off Bridge River from its ancient bed and diverted it through the mountain, also drowned the few farms in the valley. There used to be homes there, and fields and barns, horses and cattle; for where there was land, however remote, the settler came. It is one long hill down to the lake and then the road passes through a tunnel and over the dam where the road forks, left, to Bralorne and Pioneer mines, right, down the empty river canyon to Lillooet 30 miles distant.

The Bridge River canyon was once considered inaccessible, and it is due to the initiative of the miners that a road was eventually put through. The inhabitants of the mining community on the upper reaches of the river had long been frustrated by the lack of direct road communication with outside points. They had to drive over the mountain to Shalalth and load their cars on the P.G.E. — when it was running — to travel to Lillooet and further. They eventually tackled the canyon themselves, and drove a road through by blasting and undercutting the vertical cliffs. It is a very deep and narrow gorge rendered quite awesome by the tremendous rock cliffs that stand almost perpendicular on each side of the river bed.

It is practically a dry bed now, for the only water in it comes from a few small creeks below the dam. This insignificant stream trickles through a waste of boulders polished and carved by aeons of river action. When the water was first cut off jade hunters and prospectors had a field day, but the bed is growing up to cottonwoods now, and there are no more spring floods to stir up the boulders.

Where the Yalakom River comes in with a flurry of foam the road climbs to the benches and continues through rugged and parklike country where the widely and evenly spaced pines leave plenty of scope for sumac and juniper. The canyon is wider now, and where the river has cut down through thick beds of gravel the relics of older placer workings may be seen. Old log buildings and fences in isolated pockets signify native homes where a trickle of water makes possible the irrigation of a garden or small hayfield; and the occasional creek, Applespring, and others curiously named, raise visions of fertility, could the predominating rock be exchanged for soil.

Lillooet is old, and time has left many of the buildings in the vicinity undisturbed. I have known those who have claimed for their log houses a hundred years — needlessly though, for the buildings themselves spoke the truth. At the junction of Bridge River with the Fraser on a high bench stands a native village, deserted for many years, although the picturesque old church is still used on occasion. (This church has since been destroyed by fire.) A number of old, sturdy log buildings remain, weathered almost to the colour of the surrounding rock, completely integrated into a landscape that only Lillooet can provide.

Here you can savour Lillooet. Below you the Fraser swirls and eddies, and Bridge River comes in through a narrow rock trench which at one time was a mass of foam but now contains only a feeble stream. Across the Fraser the P.G.E. again comes into view, toiling up the canyon wall in its terrific climb to Kelly Lake. You see the spindly shelters of Indian fishing camps, smell the scent of the sage, hear the rocks loosened by the wind rolling down gravelly slopes. Within a mile or so from this place you will hit paving, and soon the road swings away from the canyon on to the broad bench where the old town sits in the sunshine. The journey is about 170 miles — it seems more.

SOME LILLOOET BYWAYS

All Lillooet roads are byways really, apart from the sleek, forty-mile stretch of highway connecting that town with the Trans-Canada Highway at Lytton. This highway is a modern thing, though, an upgrading of a road which through most of Lillooet's history had all the attributes of a byroad. It was a very exciting one too, for it penetrated in its rough and crooked way a country of rugged beauty steeped in memories. No interior town has more impressive approaches than Lillooet. The drive from Lytton opens up a succession of mountain views and canyon scenes, generally from elevated viewpoints, for the road follows the benches which are of considerable height above the river.

The primitive nature of the old road can be judged by the occasional sections of by-passed track that wriggle around deep gullies and between rocky outcrops, obstacles that the early road-builders took seriously enough to detour whenever possible. There are still some sections where the modern road shrinks to fit the stature of the old, to skirt some rock bluff where the terrain still outwits the engineer, but generally the route is wide and smooth, swooping and climbing, swooping and climbing, after the fashion of the Hydro transmission lines that accompany it part of the way.

This road shrinks again to fit the narrow suspension bridge that has been Lillooet's connection with the outside world since a ferry served that purpose long ago. The antique span, seeming too slender for modern traffic, bridges the rocky gorge of the Fraser and gives access to the western bench which is the only really adequate site for a town in all the canyon between Hope and Soda Creek.

To the confirmed highway traveller who is loath to venture off paving, Lillooet is the end of the road, and unavailable to those who follow main travel routes, confining their hurried explorations to the sights encountered while "passing through." The inhabitants regret this, and look forward to the time when a western route will be upgraded to a stage where it will be possible for such tourists to pass through Lillooet. But their own movements are by no means restricted to the highway which offers such a smooth and speedy egress from their mountain fastness. Trails of long ago have evolved into roads; the pack-horse has been ousted by the truck and automobile, and it is now possible to reach previously inaccessible canyon benches, drive up mountains, penetrate rocky gorges, and follow the audacious roads of the loggers to new and more exciting heights.

The builders of the first Cariboo Road set a pattern which subsequent engineers have been constrained to follow, for no deviations from the old route are apparent. This remarkable road climbs out of the bottom of the canyon from the old suspension bridge and toils steadily up the east side of the gorge, trailing like a crooked thread through an immense landscape of rock outcrops, gravel banks and sagebrush; passing the Indian villages of Fountain and Pavilion, and zig-zagging up the steep side of Pavilion Mountain to cross its flat top and plunge precipitously down to Kelly Lake on the other side. A traveller of 1863, Dr. Cheadle, described in his journal a stage trip over this road from Lillooet to 47-Mile House (Clinton) and related how the passengers walked straight up the steep face of Pavilion Mountain to relieve the overloaded horses that hauled the stage up the many switch-backs to the summit. Cheadle described the

The Fraser at Lillooet. The old suspension bridge is Lillooet's only easy road connection with the outside world.

Ponder's store at 14 Mile on the old Cariboo road as it was in 1955 (Store later burned and site abandoned). Big rock marked the site of old-time freighter's camp ground — first day's haul from Lillooet.

descent from Pavilion Mountain to Kelly Lake as "the most dangerous carriage road I ever saw." The mountain, he says, was "terrifically steep" and they "rattled down at a fearful pace." Motorists today can experience similar sensations when travelling this same road, but many of the sights Cheadle saw have passed away, and the road houses he mentioned are no longer to be seen. He passed the famous (some would say notorious) Judge Begbie on horseback, and later a "magnificent camel" grazing beside the road.

Many of the landmarks on this historic road have succumbed to the natural effects of weathering and the demands of road improvements. Log buildings disappear through various causes, and even the last decade has seen the removal of a number of these weatherbeaten cabins.

Old stone walls that once bordered the road across the Fountain flats yeilded to progress and are now, presumably, incorporated in the roadbed itself. Cheadle's journal reflected the physical trials of the road and the hardships of the primitive accommodation for travellers. He spent the first night from Lillooet at 15-mile, a short stage after a late start and with a heavy load. The first stage for freight-haulers was at 14-mile where a small creek supplied water. Until recent years a huge, smooth boulder marked the site. It was blackened at the base by many campfires and carried the prominent inscription "Camp Ground." This relic has been shoved aside and nearly buried as a result of road-widening activities.

Another traveller on this road, in the nineteen-twenties — too late, of course, to encounter camels, and judges on horseback — was impressed by the wild beauty of the scenery, which Cheadle briefly referred to as "Fraser River scenery." Lukin Johnston, a hitch-hiking journalist who travelled the interior byways, described the view of the junction of Bridge River and the Fraser from the road four miles out of Lillooet as "one of the most perfect views in British Columbia." The road is a thousand feet above the junction, and one looks down on seemingly toy houses in the deserted village at the confluence. Johnston, as he travelled up this road to Pavilion, noticed the little ranches revealed by the green, irrigated benches far away on the opposite side of the canyon. This was the roadless side where thin trails etched across precipitous slopes enabled the sure-footed pack-horses of the canyon dwellers to travel from ranch to ranch, and after many miles to Lillooet.

The main trail on this mountainous west side started at the deserted village at the junction of Fraser and Bridge Rivers a few miles from Lillooet and ran north to Empire Valley where a short stretch of road continued to Gang Ranch, a total distance of about 70 miles. Here and there along the trail, usually many miles apart, were small ranches where some mountain creek permitted the irrigation of the benches high above the river gorge. Ranchers along the northern reaches of the trail had an outlet to civilization in the ferry at Big Bar Creek which transported livestock, supplies and equipment across the river, and made contact with an actual road which climbed out of the canyon and wandered across the plateau, eventually reaching Clinton forty miles to the east.

I rode this trail in 1930 when travelling from the Chilcotin to Lillooet, having been directed to it by cowboys at Gang Ranch who assured me it was a much shorter trip than the roundabout way by road. They were right, but from them I got no inkling of the thrills involved in the passage of the route. The journey introduced me to some of the roughest sections of the Fraser Canyon where the country appeared to be all standing on end and no level land was to be seen. The trail traversed razor-backed ridges, descended abruptly into deep gullies, and climbed again up hills so steep that I was forced to relieve my saddle horse of my weight. I spent a night with a homesteader whose hayfield was a steep bench sloping down to the brink of a vertical cliff which saved him the trouble of fencing. His home was a dirt-roofed log cabin perched precariously on the hillside. Although he had lived in the canyon for a long time he seemed to have but a hazy idea of how far he was from civilization. He thought he was 90 miles by trail from Lillooet, a ridiculous estimate as he assured me he had once ridden the distance in a day. Proceeding next day I passed a large band of sheep a few miles along and enquired of one of the sheep-herders the distance to Lillooet. He told me 45 miles, but his partner a couple of miles further along informed me that it was no more than 25 miles to my destination. The closest estimate of this trail was made by a rancher in

Empire Valley who judged it to be 60 miles. Apparently the hermits who used the trail had each his own particular estimate of a canyon mile.

During the whole three-day trip from Gang Ranch to Lillooet I passed, apart from the sheepherders, only one other traveller on this trail — a prospector with several pack-horses heading north from Lillooet to Chilcotin.

Once I got off the track. It was on a low stretch where the trail descended almost to river level, and drifting sand blown by the constant canyon wind had quite obliterated it. I saw a hill trail leading steeply upward and followed it for a few miles, coming eventually to a tiny ranch in an elevated pocket of the hills. The rancher and his wife, surprised and pleased to see another human, invited me to rest my horses and share their mid-day meal. Later they directed me to a "short cut" by which I regained the trail. I remember passing another isolated ranch were a cavalcade of dark-eyed children escorted me, laughing and chattering, through the sagebrush for a short distance.

The few little homesteads and ranches I passed on this trail had the unmistakable look of old-established places, and I know now that these remote canyon benches have been occupied for more than a century. Now the road is creeping north from Lillooet, following generally the meanderings of the old trail, and a few ranchers up to 30 miles in have hung up their pack-saddles and are going to town in cars and trucks. The Thomas Johnsons, 28 miles in, moved to their canyon ranch six years before the road was made so they know something of the charms of solitude. Their log house is thought to be more than a century old, and it certainly looks it. At one time it was occupied by Chinese who irrigated the benches, grew vegetables and raised pigs which they moved over the trail to Lillooet. The place became known as the China

Ranch. The Johnsons have unearthed opium pipes and other relics while cultivating their garden.

When the Johnsons came in the old trail northward had been improved to the stage where it was possible to get a caterpillar tractor over it, so they brought their equipment in via Big Bar ferry, 30 miles up the canyon, and hauled it by cat over the trail. In the old days farm machinery was brought into this rough country in sections on pack-horses, and the fat cattle of the ranchers driven out over the same trail. The Johnsons raise two crops of alfalfa hay on their benches which are well supplied with water from a creek. Their herd of 160 head is ranged on Hogback Mountain 20 miles away, and in the fall pastured on the aftermath of the hay fields. Winters are short in the canyon, and the snowfall light, so the hills and benches are usually clear by early March. It's a pretty good place for wintering cattle.

You can grow any kind of vegetable in the canyon provided you have water. That indeed is the limiting factor, for the region lies well within the interior dry-belt. Each isolated green patch depends on a mountain creek because the benches as a rule are much too high above the river to make water from that source even a remote possibility. From some of these hay fields you can look almost straight down on the Fraser far, far below.

The construction of the road made a considerable difference to the Johnsons' way of life. Their son and daughter were able to attend school at Lillooet where they boarded, coming home to the ranch on week-ends, and the fall calf crop could now be trucked down to Lillooet 28 hair-raising miles away, for the road has most of the spectacular qualities of the old trail. It turns off the Bridge River road three miles from Lillooet — the sign says Slok Creek Forest Development Road — and climbs steeply to the bench where the remains of a deserted village sit forlorn now among the sagebrush. There is a story that the village was depopulated by an influenza epidemic — Lukin Johnston says in 1918 — but when I rode through in 1930 there were people living in it. George James, an Indian who claims to have been born in the village in 1895, says there was no water at all in the settlement, and every drop used had to be laboriously carried up the steep and gravelly hill from the river several hundred feet below. It is probable that this factor was chiefly responsible for the abandonment of the site. The recent burning of the church removed one of Lillooet's most interesting landmarks, but the well-stocked cemetery on the edge of the bench remains as proof of the village's former populous state.

The road continues along the rocky canyon of the Fraser until an immense rock bluff bars the way. Here the steep climb up the mountain commences, zig-zag fashion, to get above the obstacle, and the road proceeds at a high level, thus avoiding the impossible cliffs of the gorge. This lofty track opens new vistas in a canyon otherwise traversed at more moderate heights. Most of the vast landscape is below the observer, like a huge physical map with the prominent ribbon of the Fraser dividing it. On either side of the river gorge the benches commence, and green patches here and there show where the clever canyon people have conducted water to a deposit of good agricultural soil. The green patches, however, are but minor features in the immense landscape. They serve to demonstrate the scarcity of water in this arid land, for the benches themselves are quite extensive. Careful scrutiny of the scene will perhaps reveal faint parallel lines across these sagebrush wastes, the unmistakable traces of abandoned irrigation ditches; and a closer study through binoculars will almost certainly discover a mouldering heap of logs that was once a cabin, and possibly the straggling relics of old log fences.Such relics suggest that human activity was once more evident on the roadless

View of the Fraser from the Slok Creek road which replaced early trail to remote west side ranches.

side of the canyon than it is today, and the dust of riders passing over the precipitous trails a more common feature of the summer scene.

This high view from the Slok Creek road, which reaches heights that the old trail never attained, lays the opposite side of the canyon out like a plan, and the observer sees, far away, the wriggly line of the old Cariboo Road traversing the mountain range which confines the canyon. Another line is seen, but straight as if laid on with a ruler, sloping steeply up to a gap half way up the mountain range into which it disappears. Too steep to be a railroad, you say, but it actually is — the famous P.G.E. (now British Columbia Railway.) From this vantage point you can watch a train, five locomotives and a hundred cars, toiling slowly up the incredible grade from Lillooet to Kelly Lake. By looking almost straight down on his own side the observer may spot the roofs of the little Blue Ridge school and teacher's cabin — no longer in use since the coming of the road — far below in a little pocket in the mountain, and yet a long distance above the river gorge. One wonders whence came the pupils and how many mountain miles they had to ride to reach their isolated school.

A MOUNTAIN EXCURSION

The Okanagan Valley marks the eastern limit of the dry-belt, and beyond that the timbered ridges of the Monashee Mountains and the green valleys of the Arrow Lakes, the Slocan and Kootenay Lake country bespeak a region of heavier precipitation. The dense forest growth covers all but the most precipitous mountains up to timber-line which is about 6,000 feet, and clothes the valleys too, down to the edge of every lake and stream. The valleys are narrow, the mountains steep and high, carrying permanent snow which is always an asset to a summer landscape; and the roads that take their sinuous course in and out among the mountains lure one on, presenting cool and refreshing scenes at almost every turn.

Our base at Armstrong puts us within easy reach of this intriguing region. We could travel east over the Monashee road to Upper Arrow Lake and the Slocan, or via Revelstoke and Arrowhead to the fascinating Trout Lake and Lardeau country. We made many trips, enticed by the peaceful scenes and quiet roads, few of which could pretend to the status of a highway, some indeed being mere rough tracks up mountains like the one described in the following story.

While lying on the hot pebbles of the beach at Slocan Lake we could see the tower and summer home of the Forest Service lookout man perched on the sharp summit of Silver Ridge, also known as Idaho Mountain, more than 6,000 feet above the level of the lake. The tower, which in the distance appeared as a tiny white speck against the blue sky, stood above the extensive snow-drifts which still occupied the northern slopes and hollows of the mountain; and the July sun, a month past the solstice, beat down with its accustomed intensity on lake and snow-drifts alike. My daughter, Griselda, swam lazily back and forth in the deep water off shore. Spring seemed a long time past. There had been a full term of school since Easter, and now summer holidays were well advanced; the cherries were ripe and the grain fields in the valleys were starting to turn yellow, giving the cultivated landscape the patchwork quilt appearance usually associated with harvest time. And yet, the lookout man on the mountain was watching the snow-drifts melt and the resurgent buds push from the naked earth.

The local forest ranger reported the mountain accessible by the rough road, which by a circuitous route climbed to within a mile or two of the peak. His description of the alpine country above the timber in the full flush of spring was so alluring that we decided to drive up and see these wonders. So, early next morning soon after the sun had peeped down into the little town of New Denver where we were staying, we started up the road.

Road is, perhaps, too flattering an appellation for the track that zig-zags from the base of Silver Ridge up to timber-line. A little narrower would be too narrow, a little steeper would be too steep, and the hairpin bends only just allow a car to squeeze around. Such a road traverses in a dozen miles climatic zones representing hundreds of miles of latitude in flat country. Accustomed to travelling over these narrow tracks, the residents of the Slocan use them regularly as they find them convenient for reaching the higher elevations where they like to go to gather huckleberries in season, and walk among the wild flowers in the belated alpine spring.

A rest in the "Basin" while climbing Idaho Mountain.

So we courageously started up the road, passing first through gloomy woods of hemlock, fir and cedar, so dense that the sun never penetrated to the forest floor, which was carpeted with luxuriant mosses, and spangled here and there with the white flowers of bunchberry. Twin flower, queen's cup and other shade-loving plants grew among moss-covered fallen logs, and rich clumps of ferns raised their delicate fronds towards the equally delicate fronds of the hemlocks. Occasionally bright cascades of clear water came foaming down the steep to boil under crude log bridges and continue headlong down to the valley. With the ascent the character of the forest changed. It became more open and at intervals glimpses of the valley and the opposite peaks could be had. The trees, too, were different. Cedar and hemlock were no longer to be seen, and birch also, which grew among the conifers on the lower slopes, had disappeared. Spruce and lodgepole pine were now in evidence, and when the first balsam fir was encountered we knew that we had climbed to an altitude greater than four thousand feet.

The thinning of the forest permitted other forms of vegetation to flourish, and here the mountain shrubs came into their own. Most noticeable, the white rhododendron occupied patches of rocky ground between clumps of trees with its close companion, the huckleberry, which is equally at home high or low on the mountain. At these higher elevations where the forest is losing its hold the shrubs grow in tangled masses, clothing the landscape with a lighter green and reaching upward until they, too, pass their limit of maximum growth and begin to fail and become stunted. As the forest below gave up its struggle against the increasing inhospitality of the higher regions so do the shrubs in their turn; they gradually dwindle, giving way to hardier plants, the short grasses and the heathers, above which only lichens are able to exist.

It is in the zone above five thousand feet that the alpine spring exhibits its greatest charms. Here, under the influence of the hot sun of late July, many flowers spring up in the wake of the retreating snow-drifts, and the upper slopes of the mountains are transformed into huge flower gardens. At this height the forest, being near its upward limit, is beginning to break up into clumps and islands of dwarfed but hardy balsam; open, grassy spaces appear, growing larger with increasing elevation until they merge into the final upland of rock, turf and heather.

Such is the country to which we came at last — not without some feelings of relief — having successfully negotiated the narrow mountain road which now emerged from the last stand of timber into a cirque, a hollow produced by a former glacier. Known to the natives as The Basin, this great amphitheatre offered the first level ground we had encountered on the ascent of the mountain, but as we at this moment found the road partially buried under snow we were forced to leave the car and continue the climb on foot.

As nearly the whole basin was covered with flowers Griselda was able to collect specimens as we went along, and soon she was joyfully exclaiming as she discovered strange blooms. Among the flowers she collected and identified were, glacier lily (Erythronium grandiflorum Pursh) growing in the greatest profusion throughout the cirque, its yellow blooms tinting the landscape and crowding to the very edges of the snow banks; alpine anemone (Anemone drummondii) in clumps and patches here and there among the rocks; the spring beauty (Claytonia lanceolata Pursh) — also known to the valleys where it blooms in early March — looking very shy and timid in such gay company; red monkey flower (Mimulus lewisii) lining the banks of small watercourses and looking like a fugitive from some exotic garden; and the Menzies beard tongue (Penstemon menziesii) a dwarf penstemon of great beauty clinging to rocks in drier situations. Also collected but not identified were two flowers partial to wet ground, a handsome anemone-like flower growing in water, and a bright yellow ranunculus or buttercup rendered all the more interesting because of its comparative rarity.

Although we were now high on the mountain we still could not see the summit. The steep sides of the cirque ended in a crescent-shaped ridge which we had to gain before we could see above and beyond. The road zig-zagged up the slope but it had become impossible for vehicles. However, it made an easy trail to walk on, and the slow rate forced upon the walkers by the steepness of the grade provided all the more opportunities for admiring the view which expanded at every upward step.

One aspect of mountaineering had been brought rather forcibly to our attention soon after we arrived at timber-line. On leaving the car we were attacked by large horse flies, or bulldog flies, as they are called by prospectors and others whose business takes them into the high country, and for the rest of the ascent we were continually harassed by these pests. Their bite is quite severe, so exclamations of pain and annoyance are not infrequently heard when a party is on the heights in hot weather. The flies on the mountain are sometimes so aggressive that the deer are driven to cover and remain during the heat of the day ensconced in the densest balsam thicket they can find. Prospectors build wigwams of fir branches down in the timber for their horses to retreat to when the flies are bad, and the sagacious animals soon form the habit of trotting down from the alpine pastures early in the day to take refuge in the cool, dark shelters until sunset, when the flies retire.

So we climbed higher, through the heather, slapping at the flies, until we attained the upper edge of the cirque which proved to be the backbone ridge of the mountain. The end of the road had been passed and we now followed a trail which, still trending upwards, led us towards our objective, the lookout tower. Being now in a very elevated situation — it was like walking along the ridge of a steep-roofed house — we could look down on both sides of the mountain; we found that the southern slope was completely free of snow, in great contrast to the northern approach up which we had made our way. The greatest accumulation of snow lay along the northern side of the ridge just below the crest.

A stiff south breeze had greeted us as we emerged from the shelter of the cirque, and it continually swept the ridge, alleviating somewhat the attacks of our enemies the flies, but doing nothing to help us preserve our precarious balance. A mile of trail along the ridge brought us at last to a view of the peak which was marked by the little white tower of the lookout man on the very apex. The sight of our objective encouraged us to greater effort; the last steep pitch was overcome, and we arrived panting on the peak, to be greeted by a hospitable sign welcoming us to Idaho Lookout, 7,476 ft. The youthful lookout man, Fred Kanigan, held the door of his tiny castle open so we could enter quickly and take refuge from the flies.

Griselda was now able to look down on Slocan Lake, more than a vertical mile below, and see the white line that marked the beach off which she had been swimming the day before. The view was magnificent, and Fred was constantly looking at it, with a professional eye of course, for his duties as a watchman required him to be always on the alert. He must report by radio any fresh smoke he detects in the great landscape under his surveillance. Fred told us his supplies were brought up the trail from the end of the mountain road by means of a remarkable machine which he described as a self-propelled wheelbarrow. It had been introduced to do away with the heavy labour of back-packing, an old-fashioned activity universally practised by the early prospectors but no longer in vogue in this mechanical age.

Naturally, the most prominent mountains are selected for the sites of lookout towers, so you may be sure that when you visit one you will have an unobstructed view in every direction. Idaho Lookout is outstanding in this respect, so Fred's binoculars were passed around and we studied the surrounding peaks and the valleys between them; the old mines that were visible here and there almost to the tops of some mountains — for the Silver Slocan is riddled with the tunnels of former mines and prospects — and the details of the little town of New Denver so far below the peak, occupying the alluvial fan that projects into the fiord-like lake. Glaciers and

The lookout on Idaho Mountain comes into view beyond a big snow-drift.

snowfields were inspected, and the bright creeks and cataracts trailing from them into the wooded valleys below. At last the declining sun reminded us that it was time to start the descent. Loath to go, and rather envying Fred his situation, we at last started down, gathering specimens of heathers and flowers on the way and still subjected to the attacks of the bulldog flies. Reaching the bottom of the basin we continued our downward course by car and were soon descending steeply through the timber. Down through the spire-like balsams into the dark, dense forest, the banks of fern, the luxuriant moss, the pale bunchberry flowers, the cascades of water dropping from the snowdrifts we had so recently traversed; down into the delicate greenery of the hemlocks and cedars where the road is a mere tunnel in the gloom and the warm air seems stifling after the fresh breezes of the peak. Down at last to the hurrying creek, swollen with melted snow, filling the narrow gulch with its commotion, and finally, down to the quiet lake where once again Griselda swims back and forth off the warm beach.

The valley is now in deep shadow but sunset lingers on the peaks, and the tiny white speck that is the lookout shows boldly against the evening sky. All agree that, with the possible exception of the flies, it has been a perfect day.

IN THE LARDEAU COUNTRY

Hidden away between glittering mountain ranges, remote from the major travel routes, the sequestered ghost towns of the Lardeau country decline in picturesque decay, almost reclaimed now by the prosperous forest growth encroaching on the man-made clearings of seventy years ago. Strange, that in a country so rich in scenic attractions towns should waste away, railroads vanish, and the rank undergrowth of lush forests, the cow parsnip and devil's club, invade the precincts of once flourishing communities, overgrowing roads and the foundations of ruined buildings, burying rusted machinery and hiding the tracks and trails over which the prospectors moved, confident that they had the world by the tail.

The proposition: "You can't live on scenery," generally accepted (except by real estate men) has special significance in the Lardeau country, for when the mines faded there was nothing to replace them and the nature of the country denied the prospectors even the opportunity of growing their own beans.

With the exception of a few acres of river flats at Beaton there is no agricultural land in the Lardeau. It is a country of steep mountains overtopped by snow peaks and glaciers dribbling icy streams down through dense forests of fir, cedar and hemlock second only in size to Coast timber, to issue in one clear river of purest water, the sparkling Lardeau, most northerly feeder of Kootenay Lake. Today this wild landscape is somewhat modified by logging operations with the usual devastation of slash and scarred mountain-sides, but the snow peaks are pure as they ever were, enticing the traveller on with each fresh glimpse.

Two routes lead into the Lardeau country — three, if you count the one that comes in by the back door. [This was written before the flooding of the Arrow Lakes and the Columbia Valley forced the rerouting of some roads.] From the south the road from Nelson running north along the west side of Kootenay Lake through Kaslo is paved as far as Duncan Dam, and continues into the Lardeau, a gravel road closely following the river. The northern entry is the old route via Arrow Lakes ferry. From Revelstoke on Highway 1 the road — mostly gravel — runs south to Arrowhead, crossing the Columbia River twice by free ferry. At Arrowhead, crossing of Upper Arrow Lake is made by ferry, daytime only, every hour, to a point designated as Galena Bay. This sets the traveller down on a vacant shore with only a gravel road heading off into the bush. But it leads on, hopefully, with devious windings, as if it can't make up its mind as to its destination. A couple of miles from the ferry landing this road forks, the left fork leading to the Lardeau and the right proceeding towards Nakusp. This is the back door route, so called because it is a rough and ready road. It was punched through in a hurry a few years ago when the Nakusp-Arrowhead ferry was permanently suspended, and now provides a tenuous connection between the two points. The last time I used it it wasn't bad but recently some Lardeau hermits complained of it being rough, and their judgement should be taken seriously indeed.

However, it provides a fairly direct access to the Lardeau for travellers coming over the Monashee road from Vernon to Nakusp, and the forty-odd miles of shaking and rattling should be undertaken in a spirit of gratitude for the privilege of gaining entry to such a delightful region.

This northern entry introduces the tourist immediately to one of the chief charms of the Lardeau: its quiet and peaceful atmosphere, the feeling of remoteness from the bustle and pressures of civilization that settles like a benediction over the whole area. Along the quiet road the pleasures of country travel may be experienced to the full. The occasional cold creek offers relief and the opportunity to picnic even on the hottest days. Backward looks from elevated points reveal an unusual skyline in the steep rock towers and buttresses of the Monashee Mountains standing high on the far side of Arrow Lake. Actually, this little road from Galena Bay inland to where it intersects the Beaton-Trout Lake road about twelve miles distant is comparatively recent, the original point of entry being Beaton at the head of the northeast arm of Upper Arrow Lake, a twelve mile ferry trip from Arrowhead. At the intersection of the roads Beaton lies to the left, all steeply downhill, the track down to it being a very interesting example of what the maps of 1930 classed as main roads.

Beaton's quiet decay has been rudely hastened by the Columbia development program which calls for the raising of the level of Arrow Lakes by forty feet. This will flood most of Beaton. The present clearing, and wrecking of old buildings, is mopping up the relics fast. Gone already are church and school and many old homes. Fred Lade, a pioneer who arrived in the Lardeau at the age of ten, acquired one of these buildings and moved it log by log up the hill where he is building himself a home. The cedar logs are perfectly sound after sixty years of service. Fred says he's happy to be in Beaton now after an unwilling exile of many years from the Lardeau. He returned only last spring [1967] at the age of 74, glad to shake the dust — or rather, the dew — of Vancouver off his feet, and enthusiastically undertook the building of a new home well above the projected flood line.

Old-timer Fred Lade drove a stage between Lardeau mining camps as a youth, and has many tales to tell of the old mining days. He is now one of the few inhabitants of Beaton.

Owing to the current activity in logging Beaton's present population is about forty, but in the neighbouring mining camp of Camborne, eight miles up the Incompleux River, no one remains. Camborne, though, is better preserved, having had a period of more recent activity following the reopening of the Meridian mine in the nineteen-thirties. The mill of the Sunshine-Lardeau mine looks stout enough to go into operation today, and of course the local talk is that there is plenty of ore yet, just waiting until metal prices reach the profitable level. Fred Lade says he wouldn't advise anyone to try the Camborne road now. Part of the way goes through the startling canyon of the Incomappleux and is built up with trestle work against the sheer walls, with the river just boiling beneath. According to Fred one of the stringers has gone out, rendering the track unsafe. It's a pity because it was a most picturesque drive, the vertical canyon wall green with moss and maidenhair fern, and the white water seething below.

A report of 1903 lists Camborne's population as 500, and describes the camp as: ". . . only 3 or 4 years old but having several comfortable hotels, stores, livery stables and a post office." At the time there were three mines with stamp mills ready to go into production. A later report, 1907, says: "hard times loomed," and by 1909, "all the gold properties idle," and, "The history of the gold camp is a sad one, much money has been spent and little obtained in return." The first gold claim staked in the Camborne camp was the Eva, in July, 1899.

It was the silver boom of 1895 that brought the prospectors swarming into the Lardeau, no doubt hoping to duplicate the rich and numerous finds in the neighbouring Slocan district. But the Lardeau never equalled the Slocan in the richness of its mines, although its ores carried gold values either as the principal metal or supplementary to silver and lead. The impression is inevitable that more money was brought into the Lardeau than taken out, and the rapid development of communities like Camborne, Ferguson and Trout Lake City was due to the feverish activity of prospecting and mining development rather than the natural growth attendant on the prosperity of producing mines. The short life of the Lardeau communities supports this view. By 1909 the boom was over and population began to dwindle.

But few mining camps completely die. There always seems to be the odd prospector sniffing about, hoping to find something the pioneers missed, and in the Lardeau the gold values in the ores stimulated a certain amount of later activity, particularly in the nineteen-thirties when some production resulted.

Many of the Lardeau lodes were near the tops of mountains. The Teddy Glacier claims, for instance, were situated at 7,800 feet, more than a vertical mile above Camborne from which they were reached by thirteen miles of steep road and pack trail. The ore on this property was first found as float at the foot of a glacier and in subsequent years was traced to the lode as the ice receded. Other elevated lodes were worked by the famous woman prospector, Mrs. Jowett, who had claims at 6,900 feet on Silver Cup Mountain near Trout Lake. The modern prospector reaches these heights with ease and comfort by helicopter but in the strenuous Lardeau days the work and expense involved in packing supplies and equipment impaired the operation of such lofty prospects.

The twelve-mile drive from Beaton to Trout Lake is notable for the groves of large cedars and hemlocks adjacent to the road, although, inevitably, they are gradually succumbing to the chain-saws of the loggers. Along the way tranquil Staubart Lake reflects the snow peaks and the forest, inviting the passing angler. Trout Lake, it seems, was noted for its fish even in the earliest times for it appears under that name in a map of 1884, long before the influx of prospectors had established the present nomenclature of the region. Trout Lake City occupied a flat at the head of the narrow, seventeen-mile-long lake and was reported to have had a population of thousands in the exciting mining days. Today it is represented by a handful of buildings, chief of which, the three-story Windsor Hotel, still retains the flavour of past times. The lusty vegetation of the region has overgrown much of the old townsite but the superb setting is unchanged, the lake stretching away in front and bright mountains with their loads of snow and ice standing high above. The convenient accommodation for summer

The Lardeau Hotel at Ferguson stands forlorn among the cow parsnip.

travellers and the spacious camping site on a flat at the lakehead provide the opportunity for a leisurely exploration of the district and perhaps to try a pan or two of gravel from Lardeau Creek. Why not? A mining publication of 1933 reports: "On Lardeau Creek 1.5 miles from the settlement, Roy Jacobson had some success in March when he recovered gold to the value of $188 in five days ..." Hans Hansen of Trout Lake worked with Jacobson at that time and has among his possessions a photograph of some of the gold taken from the claim, a beautiful assortment of nuggets arranged on a dark cloth, a collection said to total 34 ounces.

Nearby Ferguson, perhaps the ghostliest ghost town of them all, paradoxically still possesses an active post office. But it is the only inhabited building in the old town. Situated four miles up a mountain road from Trout Lake City it sits aloof from the single route through the Lardeau country, quietly savouring its lonely fate. Ashes to ashes! With every passing year Ferguson becomes smaller. Buildings collapse and the remains are burned. The cow parsnip, eight feet tall, invades the foundations, flowing in to hide the flattened houses and the scraps of machinery scattered over the site. Poles with broken wires attached stand at every angle but the perpendicular, and, strangely, persist the flowers of forgotten gardens, sweet aliens almost smothered by the indigenous growth.

The heavy snowfall of the region is hard on the old buildings. Unless relieved of the weight they crumple under the load, and spring finds them a heap of rubbish with pitiful scraps of furniture showing among the ruins. Little of Ferguson remains today. Out of five hotels only one still stands, and its years are numbered. Last winter the verandahs — rich with gingerbread — of the old Lardeau Hotel caved in under the weight of the snow and now lie, an untidy heap of debris, in the overgrown road.

In the mining days Trout Lake City depended on water and rail transportation for its southern communications. A C.P.R. steamboat navigated Trout Lake to railhead at Gerrard where freight and passengers were moved by train to the port of Lardeau near the head of Kootenay Lake, from which point the steamboat was again resorted to for the passage to Nelson. Fiord-like, Trout Lake offered more inducements to navigators than road builders, but when steam went out of fashion a road was devised along the steep mountain-side high above the water. It is narrow and crooked, but adequate for today's intermittent traffic in the area. It is also a scenic delight, for its elevated situation opens up splendid views of the

Ghost town building with roof caving in, a relic of Ferguson, Lardeau mining town now practically abandoned. Photo, 1965.

Lardeau's fascinating mountains. Numerous horseshoe bends plunge the road into deep ravines where almost vertical creeks drop through dark woods of hemlock and cedar. It is a quiet road where you can watch an unconcerned porcupine rambling along or perhaps come suddenly upon a coyote or a bear. These are the inheritors of the Lardeau after the brief occupancy of the prospectors.

A sign erected by some wag at the outfall of Trout Lake makes a suitable epitaph for the community that formerly existed there — "Gerrard, unincorporated, Pop. 1." A line of weathered piles reaching out into the lake marks the site of an early wharf, and a depressing accumulation of old lumber and parts of buildings indicate the former presence of freight sheds and other buildings connected with the railhead. The railroad grade provided a fine roadbed after the rails were taken up, making a perfectly level road all the way to Kootenay Lake. In the true Lardeau tradition the wayside ghost towns of Poplar Creek and Gold Hill hide their scanty remains among the trees. Popular Creek enjoyed a mild boom in 1903 when rich goldbearing quartz veins were discovered there less than a hundred yards from the railway but, as with all the Lardeau mines, the prospectors failed to discover large bodies of commercial ore, and without the backing of steadily producing mines the settlement declined.

Nature, it appears, has won the first round in the Lardeau country, with few scars to show for the struggle. Her powers of regeneration are vigorous but so far they have not been equal to the task of healing one notable wound inflicted by the energetic pioneers. This is a huge roadside cavern at a point previously known as Marblehead near Howser. Judging by the inscriptions on the walls every traveller stops here to marvel at the great cave virtually sawn out of the vertical cliff. It was a marble quarry, and it is the last sign of the former activities of the Lardeau men. A few miles ahead lies Duncan Dam, and, to one who has fallen under the spell of the Lardeau, regrettably, the paved road marking the approach to civilization.

REFUGEES FROM ARROW DAM

Rural change in interior British Columbia was abnormally hastened with the building of the Columbia River Treaty Dam at the outfall of Lower Arrow Lake which flooded the Columbia Valley as far north as Revelstoke, drowning the sites of many lakeside communities, covering farms and homes and the little country roads that used to wind along beside lake and river. When full, the reservoir fills the valley to a level forty feet above the previous high water of the Arrow Lakes, but the annual drawdown reduces this level considerably, leaving exposed a wide and desolate shoreline. At this low stage the whole 30-mile-long valley between Revelstoke and what was previously Arrowhead, where the Columbia River once entered Upper Arrow Lake, is a depressing mud-flat sprinkled with stumps and stranded logs. It is a dead valley, alternately flooded and indecently exposed.

Its short history of settlement ended in 1969 with the completion of High Arrow Dam, but for several years before that residents were moving out, some of them taking their houses with them, Hydro crews were clearing and burning, and the smoke of their fires filled the whole valley.

The upper valley was a gateway to the Lardeau mining country; a branch line of the C.P.R. from Revelstoke to Arrowhead moved freight and passengers to the lakehead where frequent steamboat service connected with near and distant points on the lakes. A road also rambled through the valley, linking the little settlements of Mt. Cartier, Sidmouth and Hall's Landing, and ending at Arrowhead where the motorists of later years could board the stern-wheel steamboats for the passage of the lakes. A traveller in 1904, John Foster Fraser, described a trip over the route at a time when general optimism prevailed as to the potential of the region. He travelled by train from Revelstoke to Arrowhead, his fellow passengers being mostly miners bound for the Lardeau and Arrow Lakes prospects. The 124 mile passage of the Arrow Lakes was made on the steamer Rossland, which, after many wilderness lakeside calls, delivered him at Robson. Fraser was impressed with the wild beauty of the scenery and the pioneering types, many of them old bearded fellows, who appeared out of the bush to meet the steamboat at isolated spots along the lakes.

The chapters dealing with the region affected by the Columbia River Treaty were written at different times during the transition period when new routes and communications were evolving. "Refugees from Arrow Dam" was written before the completion of the dam when the old routes through the valley were still in use.

When the Arrow Dam, important phase of the Columbia River Project, is completed the level of Arrow Lakes will be raised forty feet and the Columbia Valley flooded as far north as Revelstoke, creating a reservoir 145 miles long. There will be a general evacuation of residents, not only from locations doomed to be flooded, but also from communities that will be isolated by the rising water. Many of the people to be displaced are farmers whose land has been laboriously cleared from the dense bush and planted to fruitful orchards which, in the early and more bustling years of the century, gave to the Arrow Lakes the flavour of a western Eden. Those were the days when every little lakeshore clearing was a port of call for the regular stern-wheel steamboats that plied the lakes, and the products of those clearings, the fruit, vegetables, berries and dairy produce found their way steadily to profitable markets via the green water of the lakes.

It is curious to compare the change in attitude to water resources over the last fifty or sixty years. The British Columbia Water Act of 1909 states the priority of water use in the following order:

1 Domestic purposes.
2 Municipal purposes.
3 Irrigation of land for agricultural and horticultural purposes.
4 Industrial purposes.
5 Power, including the use of water for generating power for sale.

Apparently assured of security of tenure the clearings along the Arrow Lakes increased and blossomed for a period. Small farming communities developed and the comfortable homes of the settlers appeared along the shores. Lovers of solitude and the serenity of the beautiful valley spent their holidays camping and fishing far from urban noise and distractions. But the end of the steamboat era brought a change in the tenor of life along Arrow Lakes. No longer was the farmer able to market his produce from the beach just a short distance from his house. He had to take to the roads, which were never remarkable as highways as they trailed for many a weary and crooked mile to reach modest centres of population. The bush and the bracken began to creep back into the clearings, and some of the farmers took to logging, which has always been a pretty stable industry in the region. Today one gets the impression that farming along the Arrow Lakes is not thriving.

But it's a cruel wrench for residents of many years to be forced to leave homes and locations to which they have become attached, to seek a fresh place to live in unfamiliar

Chris Spicer, unwilling victim of Arrow Dam, in his rich vegetable field at Naksup before flooding.

surroundings, wondering at the same time whether the settlement offered by Hydro will carry them through and enable them to establish elsewhere in approximately their present circumstances. The exodus will be forced by a new development in water resources which the Act of 1909 apparently didn't foresee — storage.

Amid the general air of reluctance to move exhibited by prospective evacuees the case of O'Neil Dube, who farms in the Columbia Valley south of Revelstoke, strikes an optimistic note.

O'Neil frankly admits he'll be glad to move. It appears that the snow is getting him down. I called at his place one brilliant day in March looking for snow pictures. I found them. I also found O'Neil, after a search. He was at the end of a long narrow corridor that he had dug in the snow, looking for his root house, he said. He'd spent most of the winter shovelling, keeping communication lines open around his little group of buildings. He plans to move to the South Okanagan — Penticton. "I've seen enough snow to last me the rest of my life," he remarked, grimly. "Eighteen feet so far this winter — and more to follow."

O'Neil's farm was in fact buried. No fences showed above the heavy blanket. A couple of mounds like haystacks indicated the position of some piles of cordwood. Two near-ten-thousand-foot peaks, Cartier on one side and Begbie on the other, crowded over the valley, walling it in. Beautiful, O'Neil admitted — and he'd appreciate some photographs to remember it by.

Asaph Domke lives 14 miles south of Revelstoke on the Arrowhead road. His farm will be submerged but the buildings which are on higher ground will be above the reach of the flooding. But he has to move just the same. This is going to be a blow to Asaph for he has spent years building decorative stonework around his roadside home. He has a 200 foot stone wall fronting the road, and a large stone arched gateway. The creek which chatters by the house is confined between vertical stone walls, and a large circular swimming pool, also of stone, now serves as a sunken garden — it was full of pansies. "It's been like that," says Asaph, "since the kids grew up and went away."

The Domkes homesteaded the land in 1938 but later plans for expansion were thwarted by the proposed Columbia River development when the government placed a reserve on all affected crown lands. But the Domkes have a fine comfortable home, a far cry from the original log cabin in which they first lived. There is a well equipped shop on the farm and a lighting plant. Mrs. Domke says they have done a little scouting and her husband constantly looks out for a convenient supply of rock. Once a rock man, always a rock man, I say.

J.M. Tillen lives at Arrowhead well above the intended flood line but he has to move out with all the other residents of the community. He has a fine large home commanding a magnificent view of Upper Arrow Lake, and the country is in his blood. He doesn't want to move. He likes Arrowhead although he admits it's nothing like the place it used to be. "It was a busy place once," he recalled. "Three steamboats and several trains came in every day. At one time we had the second largest saw mill in the Dominion at Arrowhead, and several hotels. The old Union's the only one left. It's converted into a store."

The road and railroad that connect Arrowhead to Revelstoke and the outside world will be drowned and the little community will cease to exist.

Captain John Nelson lives in the doomed area at Galena Bay across the lake from Arrowhead. He's an old man now, having lived there since he acquired his property on the lakeshore 60 years ago. A foot bridge over a creek leads to a cluster of antique buildings, one of

which, having sunk into the ground, has a doorway so low that one has to stoop to enter it. The house is full of books, family pictures with the Arrow Lakes flavour, and memories. In his younger days Captain Nelson built and operated steamboats on the lakes, and one of the buildings on his farm is a complete steamfitter's shop equipped to maintain steam engines. His interest in steamboats led him to purchase the hulk of the *Minto,* last of the Arrow Lakes stern-wheelers and veteran of fifty years' navigation of those waters. When taken out of service *Minto* was beached at Nakusp with the object of preserving her as a curiosity, but local support was not adequate to sustain the project. She fell into the hands of scrap dealers who stripped her machinery. When Captain Nelson acquired the hulk, which by that time was minus even the stern wheel, he towed it up the lake to his home at Galena Bay, floating it in to his meadow on a record high water. There she sits, a forlorn-looking object indeed, paint peeling off, surrounded by rank grass, a sad relic of a doomed valley. Captain Nelson says she's been sitting on the ground so long she'll never float again.

As to how B.C. Hydro proposes to handle Captain Nelson, his treasures and his memories I don't have a clue.

(The old *Minto* did float again. When the water rose in the reservoir she came up off the meadow, and Hydro towed her out into deep water and burned her to get her out of the way — but by that time Captain Nelson was dead.)

Nakusp is a neat little town half way down Upper Arrow Lake, mostly safe on elevated ground but with a waterfront area containing saw mills and pole yards and other installations which will have to be relocated. Nearly all the farms of the district are on bench lands and will be unaffected, but a notable exception is the property of C.R. Spicer, perhaps the richest chunk of soil in the whole Arrow Lakes region.

"It's a gold mine," maintains Spicer, a look of anguish clouding his face as he surveys his coal-black acres. "it's unique in British Columbia. I've got a market for all I can grow right at my door, and practically no competition." The "gold mine" consists of ten acres of black muck soil which was originally cleared by Chinese gardeners many years ago. A system of underground drains collects sufficient water to operate twenty sprinklers, so the water goes round and round, irrigating splendid crops of vegetables and small fruits. Spicer seems to grow everything but weeds on this ten acres. Crops follow crops through the season. Successive plantings of head lettuce produce a continual harvest through the summer, and every other kind of vegetable grows to perfection. But the

171

best part of the operation is the market. The Arrow Lakes are off the main truck routes, beyond the influence of the huge trailers that haul produce from the mass-production area of the United States and swamp the local growers in the Okanagan. Spicer has things pretty much his own way. He supplies fresh produce to communities from New Denver to Edgewood, with his chief market, Nakusp, being right at his door. But he doesn't know where he's going when the rising water of Upper Arrow Lake flows over his rich black acres.

It's not only the commercial side of the move that's worrying the Spicers. Both Chris and his wife are outdoor types. They love Nakusp and the surrounding mountains. They are ardent skiers and hikers, and the interior winters with ample snow for skiing and snowshoeing suit them fine. Summer and winter weekends find them in the mountains. Their daughters, true to the family tradition, sleep outside on the porch all the year round.

"B.C. Hydro has offered to find me land near Victoria," said Chris Spicer, gloomily, "but we couldn't live there — much too civilized for us, and the climate's too soft. We like the winters at Nakusp."

As I see it the Spicers are bound to lose on the deal. With the best of their land under water their livelihood will be gone, and while Hydro can no doubt find them similar land elsewhere it can't supply a ready made market which is not subject to tough competition.

Then there are the intangible things for which there can be no compensation. Like the Spicers, many of the people to be displaced, from farmers to owners of summer cottages, are deeply attached to their quiet homeland and have no desire to abandon the familiar fields and beaches.

TROUT LAKE AND BEYOND

Due to the flooding of the Columbia Valley, road making in that area has been accelerated. The new roads are, of course, being built to modern specifications — wide, smooth, and more direct in route than the narrow tracks that gradually evolved in the extremely rugged and densely forested country. On every trip to the Arrow Lakes country we noticed stretches of the fascinating little roads being upgraded, detoured or eliminated entirely. Regretfully, we watched the little Nakusp-Galena Bay road being converted into a paved highway on which motorists flashed by "getting somewhere" instead of poking along, enjoying nature in its varying moods, stopping at waterfalls and creeks, photographing the many brightly coloured fungi that are to be seen along this route, and absorbing the sights, smells and sounds of this immense forest wilderness.

Alarmed at the rate at which our well-loved country roads were undergoing "improvement" we made as many journeys as possible to the region, finding each time new scenes and receiving fresh impressions. By this time we had moved from our Armstrong location, having sold the farm — the children being flown — and settled in the Shuswap country, a mere forty miles away, and every bit as convenient as a base for exploring the interior as our farm was. We had arrived at last at a comparatively unfettered state, freed from the daily janitorial duties of the barn and the twice-daily ministrations to our ungrateful cows. We could now make long daytrips and stay out late at night, which we often did on our excursions to the far side of the Arrow Lakes.

Trout Lake store in its mountain setting. Later destroyed by fire.

With the filling of the Arrow Lakes reservoir and the new, more direct Revelstoke-Shelter Bay road, the journey to Trout Lake became an easy, unhurried day-trip from our Shuswap home, and we were frequently enticed into those quiet mountains. One such trip suggested the following little essay — "Trout Lake and Beyond".

Travel routes in the Upper Arrow Lake country have changed somewhat since the Arrow Lakes and the Columbia Valley as far north as Revelstoke were converted into a reservoir. New roads have been constructed at higher elevations, and in the case of the Revelstoke-Arrowhead road an entirely new route was chosen. Arrowhead, of course, has disappeared, after an interesting history that began in the earliest pioneering days of the Arrow Lakes. It was a busy little port connected by rail to Revelstoke, and at one time was extremely active as supplies poured through to the mining and lumbering communities along the lakes and back in the mountain hinterland.

After the early boom subsided Arrowhead continued as a port of call for the Arrow Lakes steamers until fairly recent times. The last stern-wheeler, *Minto,* operated for fifty years on the lakes and ended her career grounded at Galena Bay opposite her old calling place where she quietly decayed until Hydro towed her out on the lake and burned her to get her out of the way. They got rid of Arrowhead too — hotels, houses, stores, saw mill, railroad, and even the quaint little church that stood on the hill well out of reach of the new water level. But the old cemetery, presumably, remains undisturbed. It was also high on the hill, pretty well overgrown with the rank bush which is a feature of this country. There it will remain, I dare say, until the growth covers it completely, hiding for ever the stones that were scarcely visible amongst the underbrush even before the evacuation took place.

And you can't make a pilgrimage to Arrowhead now. There is no longer any road. The ferry terminal was moved to Shelter Bay on the other side of the river mouth, and from there a brand new road was blasted out of the mountain flanks all the way to Revelstoke.

This is a very fine road, all 32 miles of it, paved, with a very good grade which traversed the west side of the Columbia Valley at a considerable elevation above the water, but somehow I liked the old road better. The local people didn't care for it though. They complained that it was dusty and rough, and the two ferry crossings of the river at 12-Mile and Sidmouth were time-consuming and frustrating.

To an idler like myself the old road was full of interest. There were farms with barns built as steep as church steeples to shed the heavy snow they get in that valley; and the ferries were interesting diversions to one who had no particular schedule to keep. It was fun, too, to watch the ferryman try to dodge the log bundles that floated down when the river was high. Sometimes one hit the ferry — wham! I'll admit it was a bit exasperating when the ferry was on the other side when you reached the crossing, and the ferryman had to finish his conversation with the last passenger before he came over to get you. But progress has caught up with the ferrymen; the new road has eliminated the two river crossings, and a new and commodious craft at Shelter Bay makes the crossing every hour on the hour in the daytime.

I was going to Trout Lake, having driven down the new road from Revelstoke, and arrived at Shelter Bay on the hour to find our small car the only vehicle to board the ferry. Despite this one insignificant car on the half-acre of empty deck the imposing ferry *Galena* whistled and started the crossing just as if she had a load. It's about a twenty-minute crossing to Galena Bay, and out on the lake you get fine views of the local mountains which culminate in rocky peaks and snow. There is a choice of routes at the Galena Bay landing — south to Nakusp over a narrow but intriguing road (now, alas, being rebuilt to modern standards), and easterly to Trout Lake and eventually to Kootenay Lake and Kaslo.

I had no particular reason for this trip except that my wife said early one morning: "Let's go to Trout Lake," and as it seemed a sensible suggestion we packed up and left. That's the kind of place Trout Lake is — a place that you suddenly want to go to. It attracts me like a long-remembered homeland. It is in the mountains — real mountains with snow peaks and glaciers, and it's quiet there now, although many years ago it was the scene of frantic activity. Real towns occupied those silent woods; coaches and wagons hauled passengers and freight over

primitive roads between busy mining towns — Trout Lake City whose residents were numbered by the thousand; nearby Ferguson, four miles up a mountain track, a group of scanty ruins now; Beaton, a few old buildings left above the flood level of Arrow Lake, and Camborne hidden away at the end of a rough track through the perilous Incompleux canyon.

Old-timers still talk about the busy life of the old days, the pack-trains taking supplies up to the mountain mines, the winter activity of rawhiding out the ore, the building, the bustle and the optimism, the hotels and of course the saloons, many saloons, vouched for by the great number of old bottles lying around the overgrown townsites.

Fred Lade of Beaton can tell about the old times for he drove stage in that rough country as a youth when mining

was the thing, and the ores of the Slocan and the Lardeau attracted miners and prospectors by the thousand. It was a wild country to prospect in, as anyone can see who cares to walk a few yards off the road into the jungle-like bush, into a mess of Devil's club, windfalls and moss-covered boulders rendered half dark by the dense growth of cedar and hemlock. Fred had to come back to Beaton after most of a lifetime spent in more civilized parts, and now with his wife in a snug log house they built themselves, lives a quiet but active life. But the Beaton he knew as a youth has ceased to exist. It was just one of the little Arrow Lakes communities destroyed by the flooding.

Trout Lake itself is about 20 miles from the ferry landing at Galena Bay, on a road that is continually being improved but is still solitary enough that you might see a black bear walk out of the bush, sit down, look skyward as if estimating the time by the sun, and amble back into the bush again. The old city townsite is half lost in the bush but the odd fire hydrant tells of former streets. The operators of the fishermen's resort there, Pat and Rich Broemling, have cleared an open space to the lake which is very pleasant to walk upon and reflect upon the glory that was Trout Lake City. The Broemlings collected many relics on the site during their clearing and building operations, the hundreds of old bottles and crocks taxing the capacity of house and store where they were displayed. Their rooms shone with the lustres and colours of old glass, hand blown bottles and containers of eighty years ago, beautiful with their imperfections which the collector loves for they stamp each specimen as an individual. Some of these bottles were dug from under the roots of large trees, which indicates how rapidly the forest encroached on the dying community when the brief mining boom collapsed. (The Broemlings' fine collection was later lost in a fire which destroyed their store and home.)

The old cemetery at Trout Lake is so overgrown by the lusty vegetation of the region that it is difficult to find. It is on a bench in such thick brush that the stones and head-boards have to be sought with diligence. What legible inscriptions remain indicate that Ferguson also used this plot, for names of miners killed in the mines there are here inscribed.

The lake stretches away to the south for 17 miles, narrow, like all the lakes of these deep valleys, and flanked by wooded, snowcapped mountains which rise steeply from it. It receives the Lardeau's crystal clear water at one end and discharges it over clean gravel beds at the other, at Gerrard, another ghost town, once railhead — improbable as it seems — on a line that connected it with Kootenay Lake. Steamboats carried the traffic the length of Trout Lake in the mining days but today a road has been contrived along the precipitous mountain-side. It is one of my favourites; very narrow — wide roads don't appeal to me — crooked, ups-and-downsy and delightful. From the steep cliffs come foaming creeks, cascading to the lake a great distance below. Sluggish porcupines waddle out of your way. I don't know why they frequent this road, but they certainly seem to be more plentiful here than any other place I know.

The Lardeau River must be one of the most beautiful of streams. The sparkling clarity of the water is astonishing. Unpolluted, you say, and you can say that about all the water of this region. From the outfall of the lake the road follows the valley of this river, rarely out of sight of the eager stream, for the valley is narrow. The water is in a great hurry, sweeping noisily through bends where tangled heaps of driftwood, roots and forest trees attest the power of the river in freshet and explain the littered state of the shoreline of Kootenay Lake into which it empties. In the fall the bars of the Lardeau are white with gulls tracking the spawning kokanee, and clamoring flocks of these visitors rise as the solitary motorist surprises them. Too soon the road widens, takes on the aspect of a highway as the influence of the Duncan Dam is felt. From the head of the lake southward, construction has left a ribbon of paving to disturb the bucolic solitudes of Shutty Bench, that rare phenomenon in the Kootenays, a stretch of good agricultural land, hung, like a Swiss landscape, on the mountain-side high above Kootenay Lake.

Through a romantic countryside this smooth road leads on, sinuous, rising and descending, until with a final swoop it lands you in charming Kaslo. Its leisurely exploration is left to another chapter.

A KOOTENAY RAMBLE

"It's a wonderful sight," the woman at Trout Lake informed me. "Don't miss it on any account. Oh my, it's really something! You've just got to see the Duncan Dam."

She was quite serious, although as she spoke she stood facing a beautiful snow-clad mountain, brilliant against the soft blue background of the June sky. I actually believe she couldn't see this mountain. Being so familiar with the scene it had probably never occurred to her that the view from her door was a scenic gem of the first order. In more settled districts frontage on such a view would be worth one hundred dollars a foot. Trout Lake in June! To me this is real scenery. The sharp Kootenay peaks crown real mountains with glaciers and snowy towers putting to shame my own low Shuswapian hills. I didn't want to see any dams. I would have preferred to remain at Trout Lake, drinking it in, the scenery I mean.

I was passing through on a leisurely, unplotted ramble, enjoying the quiet and peaceful atmosphere of the district, and the realization that nature is repossessing part of her dominion once ravaged — perhaps I should say developed — by industry. The fire hydrants one stumbles over in the underbrush, the mouldering foundations, the decaying buildings, apple trees hemmed in and almost smothered by vigorous forest growth — these are comforting reminders that man's untidy activities are frequently only temporary.

It is customary to refer to settlements like Trout Lake as ghost towns, and the Kootenays hide many such places in the narrow, picturesque valleys between the mountain ranges. Mining dominated the country for a period following the discovery of rich silver-lead ores, particularly in the Slocan district, in the eighteen-nineties. The region became infested with prospectors, the mountains were riddled with holes and scarred with mine dumps, towns sprang up, railroads came into being, and steamboats puffed up and down all the lakes. Now deep silence hangs over most of the region and it is difficult to visualize the activities of the past which are vouched for, however, by old photgraphs which show clearings around towns and mine sites that are now completely covered by forest. And the quiet country roads snake through this continuous forest, brightened with tumbling creeks and green with fern and the delicate fronds of hemlock, the kind of roads along which you can loiter, enjoying the greenery, picnicking where you will, trying for trout in the creeks, meditating, botanizing, and observing the habits of mosquitoes and other larger forms of wild life. The pressures of civilization are behind you, for, strange as it seems, the tourists in general avoid the Kootenays. Perhaps the water is too cold for swimming; I think so, although several fat women I know declare it is not. But I really believe the country is too quiet for the average tourist, and beautiful scenery alone is not enough to entice him.

South of Trout Lake in the neighbourhood of the northern reach of Kootenay Lake the prevailing quiet of the country is rudely shattered. A pall of dust hangs in the air. We are approaching the vicinity of Duncan Dam — bunk houses, machine shops, trailers, trucks, earth movers, dust, noise — progress. This is the wonderful sight the woman at Trout Lake was so excited about. A road turns off and crosses a bridge over the Lardeau River. It leads to an elevated viewpoint overlooking the dam site. A large parking space has been graded to accommodate the hundreds of cars of the expected tourists, and our little

Volkswagen looked very lonesome sitting all by itself in this broad expanse. I didn't care for the view. It resembled an overgrown gravel pit with dozens of seemingly toy trucks and earth movers crawling about over the floor. The dam was beginning to rise. When completed it will back up the Duncan River and raise the level of Duncan Lake by ninety feet. The lake appears on my old map of 1884 as Upper Kootenay Lake. It is a body of water of unusual beauty set among mountains that retain much snow throughout the year. I remember several visits when these mountains were perfectly mirrored in the still water. On a last visit to this doomed lake I followed a rough road on the east side opposite the few buildings that comprise the settlement of Howser, and came to an abandoned farm, fields, orchard, log buildings and sheds, a small wharf in the bay where the farmstead was cosily situated, and many rock walls, beautifully constructed, supporting the terraced gardens of the lover of solitude who must have devoted many years to the building. Some rock flowers still bloomed on these abandoned terraces, and also along the rocky shores of the lake, sown, no doubt, by the same hand.

I read in these ruins the story of a family living in quiet solitude, close to nature, in idyllic surroundings, occupied with the seasonal tasks of farm and forest, content with the simple pleasures associated with the beautiful lake and shore, and with leisure enough to raise monuments of rock to complement the natural attractions of the site.

It is reported that clearing of the shore line is not planned at Duncan Lake so the dam will probably ruin it for recreational purposes. Is there a more desolate sight than a drowned lake ringed by the skeletons of partly submerged trees?

A further impact of the dam will be felt by the little community of Argenta, a few miles to the south. This small settlement at the head of Kootenay Lake, which includes a number of Quaker families, used to be regarded as the ultimate in isolation in this part of the province. Situated on the otherwise uninhabited side of the lake, Argenta, seen from across the lake, appears as a few small clearings at the base of a steep and high mountain range, far away and lonely. Since the end of steamboat days communication has been by a narrow road which circles the head of the lake and crosses the Duncan River by a wooden bridge. The intrepid traveller is confronted by a sign: "You are entering Argenta — are you lost or crazy?" which had real significance in the old days before the Duncan Dam brought industry and real roads to the vicinity. But despite its isolation Argenta became known far beyond its own quiet country of lake and mountain. Its small school run by John and Helen Stevenson attracted students from "outside" sent by parents wishing to have their children educated in a country environment where domestic duties were considered an important part of the students' day. "Every student has some daily task to perform," said John Stevenson. Outside students who comprise about two thirds of the enrollment are boarded with the families of the little settlement where they are assigned some household or farm duties. Argenta has the reputation of being a Quaker community but John Stevenson says this is not so, only a minority of the residents belonging to that sect. The policy of the school is, however, decided by the Friends. John and his wife are Quakers but his students might be of any religion. He said to a boy picked at random: "What is your religion, Son? — What church do you go to?"

"I don't go to any church," replied the boy.

The teachers are dedicated to rural living with its pleasures and satisfactions derived from the simple and wholesome pursuits associated with the cultivation of the soil. Modern innovations such as freezers have in no way

Approaching Kaslo from Shutty Bench, this view of the old town built on a gravel outwash is to be had.

impaired these rustic pleasures, indeed the quick and successful preservation of garden produce has encouraged the livers off the land to greater and more sustained efforts. On my visit students were sitting among the boulders of the beach — the school is near the shore just above high water line — reading for examinations. There were boys and girls from Oregon, California, Vancouver and other points in British Columbia as well as the Argenta natives. Grades 10, 11 and 12 are taught, and despite the lack of laboratories and equipment the superintendent of schools finds the Argenta students as well advanced in subjects such as physics as their better equipped urban counterparts. Actually, their studies have a practical application in Argenta where every man is his own electrician and handyman, the community generally depending on its own resources.

A new paved road all the way from Duncan Dam to Kaslo has placed Argenta within the reach of the tourist who rarely ventured there over the old rough track. Solitude is no longer easy to achieve. If, like the Argentans, you wish to retire from the world and live an idyllic life far from urban bustle, the chances are the spot you have selected will be the future site of some dam, power transmission line, pipe line or a mine. Progress will catch up with you. Other people have found this out, the denizens of Shutty Bench, for instance, whose little world occupies a steep bench above Kootenay Lake on the west side, and was for many years a quiet refuge, peaceful and remote. A sudden and recent invasion of machinery converted their crooked and narrow gravel road into a slick highway and exposed the startled inhabitants to the curious stares of hordes of construction men going to and from the Duncan Dam.

Some years ago when I first penetrated to the pastoral solitudes of Shutty Bench I encountered a man cutting green oats with a scythe and cradle. I was intrigued. My grandfather used to speak of such things but I had never seen the implement employed. I pressed on, expecting to find a party threshing grain with flails at the next homestead, but in this I was disappointed.

Shutty Bench is a unique feature of this part of the Kootenays where good agricultural soil, particularly in situations level enough to cultivate, is scarce. Some hardy settlers, it is true, have attempted farming on hillsides so steep that the rows of fruit trees stand one above the other like chickens on perches, and Shutty Bench itself is not innocent of these precipitous developments. On the whole the tract is rolling and hilly with hardly any quite level ground, and it lies like a huge green blanket along the mountain-side between Lardeau and Kaslo. It is, in fact, a little alpine world, dotted with pleasant homes, bright, flowery gardens, barns, fields and orchards. Above is the timbered steep, below, far below, the shining lake, stretching away to the south from headland to hazy headland, undisturbed now by the smudge of steamboats.

From Shutty Bench the road descends steeply to Kaslo, built on an outwash which thrusts out into Kootenay Lake. By British Columbia standards it's an old town with an interesting past. Kaslo has experienced fire and flood, boom and bust, and many of the records and relics of her triumphs and tribulations are preserved in the stern-wheel steamboat, *Moyie,* last to operate on Kootenay Lake, and now preserved and serving as a museum on the beach. I looked over the old boat and inspected the collections of relics, curious to see once more a scythe and cradle, but I found none. I suspect that some of the residents of Shutty Bench secretly use this ancient tool and are not yet ready to concede its obsolescence.

Kaslo was once the terminus of a railroad which ran back into the mountains to Sandon when that town and the intervening pass were centres of tremendous mining activity. Having a natural inclination to poking around ghost towns I took the road through the mountains from Kaslo. For part of the way it occupies the old railway grade but later climbs among the crags as a normal Kootenay road should do, passing the ruins of old mine buildings and tailing dumps. The mountains are speckled with deserted mine workings almost to their crests. Sandon is a short side trip from this road which continues to New Denver on Slocan Lake, and so narrow is the valley in which it is hidden that it is hard to believe a town so populous once stood there. Investigation, however, reveals old ruins and foundations hiding amongst the brush on the steep mountainsides. Early photographs show not only the packed buildings of the former town but the denuded mountains stripped of

Sandon City Hall after the flood which destroyed half of the old town.

timber, a common condition in old mining camps. The heart of Sandon was a double row of buildings crowded into the narrow valley bottom with the creek flowing between them, decked over with timber to form a road. Many mine dumps are to be seen at different elevations on the steep mountains above the town, and a track follows the narrowing valley beyond Sandon for a couple of miles to the site of Cody where other remains of mine buildings stand in varying stages of decay. But only a pitiful remnant of old Sandon remains today. Long after it had degenerated to the level of a ghost town a flood brought on by unusual runoff conditions washed away half the buildings and deposited them in the form of matchwood in Slocan Lake seven miles down the creek.

Sandon is still recognizable as a townsite, which is more than can be said of Three Forks a short distance down the valley at the junction of the New Denver road. Once a town of several thousand it has completely disappeared as far as the passing traveller is concerned, although if directed to the spot by a local historian one might discover the half-collapsed ruin of a building in the vigorous young forest growth. Parts of roads and railway grades can be recognized by those interested enough to thrash around in the brush, and rotting ties and timbers half buried in gravel give some hint of former construction. The flood that destroyed Sandon washed out the railway that served both towns, and turned the bed of Carpenter Creek into a waste of boulders.

Part of the fun in visiting ghost towns is to stir up an old prospector, if you can find one, and listen to his stories of the past glories of the place, any account of which is sure to include a list of the saloons that supplied the pressing needs of the community. Sandon was credited with thirteen, or was it seventeen? Three Forks had its share too. I remember the days when Three Forks had a number of large buildings and a railroad. It was reached

A relic at Cody, a mining community near Sandon.

by a different route then, on the other side of Carpenter Creek opposite the present road. This track climbed arduously from New Denver, in places a mere ledge, at dizzy heights along rocky cliffs, and it too has almost vanished. Nature is robust in the Kootenays. Slides and washouts are of frequent occurrence in these steep mountains, and any road deserted and unrepaired is soon reclaimed by the wilderness.

I overtook a prospector near Three Forks and gave him a lift to his "mine." He had driven a tunnel into the mountain from the roadside to explore a vein which the old-timers had apparently overlooked. He proudly escorted me through the workings, pointing out to me a big hole — stope, I believe, is the correct term — from which he had mined several truck loads of ore. This energetic man had located another vein in the middle of the road and planned to mine it, but the local road foreman strongly objected to the project. Apparently warm words were exchanged. The prospector related to me in vigorous language just what he'd told the road foreman. Eventually the road foreman proved victorious. The road is still there, and the prospector subsequently went away.

Perhaps the logical place to end this ramble is New Denver, built on mining and now subsisting on quiet meditation, close as can be to nature — a coyote crossed the road in front of me half a mile from town — with its back door on Slocan Lake which reaches away, fiord-like, between precipitous mountain ranges, a picture postcard town with all the components of its setting arranged as if by a skilful landscape artist. Beside the lake, on the edge of town, the old Newmarket Hotel, beautifully maintained, is a real survivor from the past, yet is strangely in keeping with the character of the town today. Old buildings and maple trees, uncrowded streets and the beautiful setting, give to New Denver an atmosphere of peace and leisure not to be found in our more populous centres.

The foregoing was written before road-making in the region had attained its present efficiency. Now many of the gravel routes which have served the country for so long have been widened and paved, and the grades in many places considerably improved. Much of the 32-mile stretch between Kaslo and New Denver is now paved, and what was once considered a rough trip can now be accomplished in comfort. The road northward from Kaslo was hastily improved to accommodate the traffic generated by the construction of Duncan Dam, but beyond that, in the Lardeau country, the quiet country roads can claim no higher status than that of byways. Kaslo has good connection with the south in the paved road to Nelson, which is now diverting tourists to the old town. Indeed, the *Moyie* steamboat's visitor's book was well filled in 1973 with several thousand names, and the old ghost town of Sandon was said to be under the constant surveillance of visitors during that same summer.